Crazy Stuff
Dictators Do

Insane But True Stories You
Won't Believe Actually Happened

Bill O'Neill

D1468754

DON'T FORGET YOUR FREE BOOKS

GET THEM FOR FREE ON
WWW.TRIVIABILL.COM

CONTENTS

INTRODUCTION

Welcome to *Crazy Sh*t Dictators Do!* In this book you'll read about some of the world's most notorious dictators, most of whom you've probably heard of before or even know a little bit about, but not in the way we're going to look at them. All of these dictators were bad and many would say evil, but they also did some truly crazy things that will make you say "WTF!"

And in most cases, the crazy stuff done by these dictators led to their demise.

All of our dictators are from what is considered the "modern" period of world history (post-1600s) because before that time most of the world's population, with few exceptions, was under the rule of kings and emperors. Additionally since there actually have been dozens of dictators in the modern era, we've narrowed our list down to ones who were notorious *and* did some truly crazy sh*t that had some long-lasting and usually negative effects.

We'll profile some "lesser" dictators who were still notorious and enacted some of the craziest policies in their countries. Ugandan dictator Idi Amin thought that he was the legitimate King of Scotland and at one point considered building a statue of Hitler. Also from the African continent, you'll read about how Yahya Jammeh instituted a policy of hunting down all the witches in The Gambia and how Francisco Macias banned fishing in Equatorial Guinea.

Needless to say, none of those three dictators got to serve out their life terms.

You'll find that the vast nation of Russia has played a major role in some of the crazy things dictators have attempted to do throughout history. Soviet dictators Joseph Stalin and Nikita Khrushchev both came up with outlandish ideas about their countries' agricultural system: in Stalin's case, it was to force farmers to work in "collectives" and in Khrushchev's, it was to attempt to grow crops in sand. Neither policy was very effective, with Stalin's policies resulting in the deaths of millions and Khrushchev's policies contributing to his removal as head of the country.

Attacking Russia also seemed like a good idea to dictators Napoleon and Hitler, but the attempts were major factors in both of their downfalls. Someone should have sent both men the memo that it'd been tried before, and failed miserably!

As you read this book, you'll see that not only does absolute power corrupt absolutely, it also makes some dictators do some truly crazy sh*t! So sit back, relax, and enjoy knowing that you aren't the victim of some of the crazy things these dictators have done.

POL POT:
LET'S ALL MOVE TO
THE COUNTRY

If there's one thing that all of the dictators in this book have in common; it is grandiosity and hubris that can't be contained.

They just don't look at the world the way most of us do, so when they see a problem, they often come up with the craziest way to solve it. And using a whole lot of crazy to "solve" a major "problem" is where we begin with our first dictator — Pol Pot.

Pol Pot was the leader of the Khmer Rouge or the Communist Party of Cambodia and eventually became that country's dictator from 1975 to 1979.

During Pot's rule—and the ten years of civil war in Cambodia and war against Vietnamese occupation that followed—between 1.5 and 2 million Cambodians were killed, or nearly 25% of its 1975 population. Some of those people died fighting, but most were ruthlessly murdered or starved by Khmer Rouge troops and followers as part of Pol Pot's grand scheme.

You see, for ideological reasons, Pol Pot decided to depopulate Cambodia's cities and make everyone become peasants. Pot's plan was to build a utopian, agrarian society, but it quickly descended into a nightmare and became the worst example of political violence and genocide since World War II.

Becoming a Communist

Pol Pot was born Saloth Sâr on May 19, 1925, in what is today Cambodia, but was then the French colony of Indochina. Life wasn't bad for young Sâr, as his father was a respected and successful farmer and his mother was a devout Buddhist. He was also educated in some of the best schools in Indochina.

It certainly wasn't the type of background one would expect for a notorious communist dictator.

Sâr's privilege allowed him to attend university in Paris from

4

1949 to 1953, where his world outlook changed dramatically. Before leaving Cambodia, most of his daily interactions were with ethnic Khmers (the term used for ethnic Cambodians) and French; although the French were always in a superior position as teachers, clergy, and government officials, military, and police. In Paris, he met people from all over the world and many French who told him that they were against their countrymen ruling his country.

The discussions at first confused Sâr, but the more he heard, the more intrigued he became. He began reading Marx and studying Lenin, although the bright but simple Sâr found the writings of Marx a bit too dense and impractical.

Sâr quickly found that Stalin and Mao were more to his liking. Probably more than anything, Sâr's sojourn in Europe influenced him to become the crazy dictator known as Pol Pot. Or maybe it just shone a light on the person he really was. Sâr wasn't interested in Marxist platitudes that could be recited for coeds at coffee shops; no, he was a man of action, just like Stalin and Mao. If Sâr could ever influence the course of his country's history, he decided that he'd do so like those two communist icons.

Sâr decided that to make the omelet of Cambodian independence, he'd have to break a few eggs!

When Sâr returned to Indochina, he worked as a teacher but devoted most of his time to activities in various communist groups in the newly independent country. He also spent a lot of time in North Vietnam, networking, and eventually fought alongside the communist forces against the Americans and South Vietnamese during the 1960s and early 1970s.

To Sâr, the spirit of a communist revolution was in the air in Southeast Asia, so in 1968, he took everything he had learned abroad and used it to launch an uprising against the Cambodian government in 1968.

Leading the Khmer Rouge (literally "Red Cambodians"), Sâr gained a reputation as a ruthless yet effective leader and by 1970 he began going by "Pol Pot." He took the name "Pol" from an ancient Cambodian tribe that fought the monarchy and "Pot" because it was a Cambodian tradition for those with no last name to make one up that sounds like the first name.

Despite American bombing raids, by 1975, Pol Pot and the Khmer Rouge had won the war in Cambodia, and in no time he set out to change the country into his vision.

The Cambodian Killing Fields

Besides being grandiose, most dictators are also extremely paranoid, usually because people *are actually* trying to kill them. In Pol Pot's case, it was others within the Cambodian Communist Party. So, shortly after officially changing the name of the country to "Democratic Kampuchea"—many dictators also have in common a desire to project to the rest of the world how "democratic" their countries are—and writing a new constitution in 1975, he turned to his enemies.

And there was no shortage of enemies: anyone associated with the former monarchy, those thought to be on the rightwing of the political spectrum, Cambodians of non-Cambodian ethnic ancestry, and any intellectuals who could question the new order.

The problem was a majority of the population could fit into any of those categories, so getting rid of them would be difficult and costly.

But then Pol Pot decided to kill two birds with one stone.

Since Pol Pot was a big admirer of Mao Zedong and the Chinese version of communism; and since the Khmer Rouge was receiving monetary support from Communist China, Pol decided to base his new vision on China's "Great Leap Forward."

Essentially, the Great Leap Forward was the Chinese government's plan to nationalize the country's farms.

Pol Pot saw this as a good idea, ideologically speaking, for Cambodia. In 1975, Cambodia was still primarily rural and most of the Khmer Rouge's support came from the peasants, unlike in more industrialized communist countries where support came from factory workers. At the same time, most of Pol Pot's political enemies were located in Cambodia's cities.

So, in what Pol Pot and probably a couple of his closest advisors thought was a flash of brilliance, he decided to totally depopulate Cambodia's cities!

The 2.5 million inhabitants of the capital city of Phnom Penh were evacuated and most of the other cities soon followed. The people of the cities were labeled "New People" and were portrayed as decadent and corrupt, as opposed to the virtuous "Old People" of the rural areas. The New People were marched and trucked to the rural areas where they were forced to work ten hours or more, seven days a week, on meager rations.

Right-wingers, former monarchists, university professors, and even people with glasses were often singled out for ridicule, physical abuse, or straight-up murder.

The fields that the New People were forced to work were places of misery, where it was common to see bodies floating in rice paddies or piled up in ditches. It's because of this that they became known as Cambodia's "killing fields."

And Pol Pot never hid from the world what he was trying to do. The Khmer Rouge had a common saying in the late 1970s directed to the New People: "To keep you is no benefit. To destroy you is no loss."

Needless to say, the New People died by the thousands, but the policy was also devastating to the Old People. In 1976, 80% of the population had malaria and the country's food supply was unable to compensate for the sudden demographic shift.

Starvation became common and dysentery was an everyday occurrence.

Things got so bad in Cambodia that Vietnam, which was also a communist country, invaded to stop Pol Pot and his crazy policy. War with Vietnam and civil war within Cambodia continued through the 1980s before finally ending in the 1990s.

Pol Pot continued to lead the Khmer Rouge from the jungles of Cambodia until he was finally turned in to the new Cambodian government by some of his own people in 1997.

On 15 April 1998, Pol Pot died in his sleep, apparently of heart failure. His body was preserved with ice and formaldehyde so that his death could be verified by journalists attending his funeral. Three days later, his wife cremated his body on a pyre of tyres and rubbish, utilizing traditional Buddhist funerary rites. There were suspicions that he had committed suicide by taking an overdose of the medication which he had been prescribed. Thayer, who was present, held the view that Pol Pot killed himself when he became aware of Ta Mok's plan to hand him over to the United States, saying that "Pol Pot died after ingesting a lethal dose of a combination of Valium and chloroquine"

There is little doubt that Pol Pot's idea of depopulating Cambodia's cities was clearly crazy and one that led to nearly two million deaths and the collapse of his government.

DID YOU KNOW?

- Sâr means "pale" or "light" in Cambodian. Pol Pot was given that name because he had a much lighter complexion than the usual brown complexion of Cambodians, perhaps due to Chinese ancestry.

- Pol Pot was married twice but only had one child.

- While the people of Cambodia were starving on meager rations in the killing fields, Pol Pot enjoyed large, multi-course meals. He was said to have a fondness for Chinese wine and cobra stew!

- Pol Pot was never a very good student as a child, but like most dictators, he had a certain amount of charisma and was said to have a keen ability to read people.

- Pol Pot died on April 15, 1998, at the age of 72, in Anlong Veng, Cambodia.

AUGUSTO PINOCHET:

FREE HELICOPTER RIDES
FOR HIS ENEMIES

As much as all dictators are infused with a healthy dose of paranoia, many of them—rightwing and leftwing—are actually pretty innovative with their methods of torture and repression. The idea of torturing or killing someone never crosses most of our minds, but dictators are a completely different breed and they tend to attract violent and often sadistic people to their circles. Often these people are more than happy to come up with new and crazy ways to dispose of their leaders' political enemies.

This was the case in Chile during most of the 1970s and '80s.

In 1973, an American backed coup d'état removed socialist Chilean President Salvador Allende from power and replaced him with a military junta that was controlled by General Augusto Pinochet. Eventually, Pinochet was made president and ruled the country with an iron fist until 1990. There were a lot of Chileans, who supported Pinochet, but there were also plenty who didn't, and if they let their opinions be known, they were subject to losing their jobs, ending up in prison, or worse...

Going for a helicopter ride!

Yes, you read that right. Pinochet's regime is believed to be responsible for the deaths of more than 3,000 political enemies and the torture of nearly 30,000. Unfortunately for the families of many of those killed by Pinochet's death squads, they were often "disappeared," which was later revealed to have been due to the death squads using helicopters to do their dirty work.

Pinochet death squads would use helicopters to transport political prisoners across the long, mountainous nation and if the prisoner was deemed too much of a problem, they'd simply throw the prisoner out over the Atlantic Ocean or in the Andes Mountains where they'd never be found.

In 1995, after death squad leader Osvaldo Romo was arrested

for his role in the helicopter rides, an interrogator asked if they always threw the victims in the ocean.

Romo replied, "I think it could have happened...Throwing them into the crater of a volcano would be better...Who'd go looking for them in a volcano? Nobody!!!"

Now that's definitely some crazy stuff only a dictator would think of.

A Military Man from the Start

Many of the dictators in our book failed in numerous professions before becoming dictators, but this wasn't really the case with Pinochet. Augusto José Ramón Pinochet Ugarte was born on November 25, 1915, to an upper-middle-class, generational Chilean family. Families such as Pinochet's were socially and politically conservative, with military service considered a rite of passage.

So young Augusto went to Chile's top military academy and entered the Chilean Army as an officer in 1935.

Also unlike many of the dictators in our book, Pinochet had no complex intellectual journey that brought him to the philosophies that drove him as a dictator. In fact, young Pinochet was relatively apolitical, which helped him progress in Chile's Army.

Perhaps somewhat ironically—or not, depending upon how you look at it—Pinochet was made the commander-in-chief of the entire army by President Allende because he was so effective at suppressing rightwing opposition on the streets.

But it was apparently all just a ruse because on September 11, 1973, Pinochet led the entire Chilean military to overthrow Allende.

In an instant, the leftwing went from rulers to the opposition and Pinochet quickly took them for a ride, figuratively and literally.

Not a Ride You'd Want to Take

As soon as Pinochet came to power, he began thinking of new ways to use normally mundane things as tools of repression. He filled soccer stadiums with political prisoners so they could be more easily processed and sent to prisons or disappeared.

His death squads also began using helicopters as their favorite type of transportation.

In the month and a half immediately after the coup, Pinochet's death squads used helicopters to transport political prisoners in what became known as the "Caravan of Death." Members of the National Intelligence Directorate (DINA) and paramilitary death squads rounded up political enemies and moved them to different prisons around the country in Puma helicopters. Nearly 100 prisoners were killed during the Caravan of Death, but it was during this time that DINA and the death squads realized that helicopters could be used in a far more nefarious manner.

So, Pinochet gave the green light for free helicopter rides for his political enemies.

Although Pinochet himself was probably never there when any of his political enemies were tossed from helicopters, his personal Puma pilot, Oregier Benavente, later admitted that he carried out several such missions.

The scope of the helicopter executions remains unknown. In 2001, Chilean President Ricardo Lagos said that 120 people were killed in such a way, but most believe the number was several times higher.

And the unique execution method proved to be so effective that it was exported.

As Pinochet became the face of anti-communism in Latin America during the 1970s, he made alliances with the rightwing and military dictatorships in Argentina, Brazil, Uruguay, Paraguay, and Bolivia. The Argentine military in particular seems to have taken the idea of "death flights" from Pinochet, as they tossed at least 1,000 of their political enemies out of planes over the Rio de la Plata outside Buenos Aries.

Pinochet's free helicopter rides were truly some crazy sh*t that had long-term ramifications for the dictator and Chilean society. After Pinochet finally handed over power in 1990, he was hounded around the world for crimes against humanity, many of them relating to the Caravan of Death, disappeared peoples, and helicopter executions.

Despite his apparent immunity due to being a former president, Pinochet also faced prison in Chile and was subject to numerous trials before he finally died on December 10, 2006, at the age of 91. Once news of the dictator's death became public, the ruptures in Chilean society from his rule became apparent.

Thousands came out in celebration of his death, but as many came to his state funeral.

Due to the crazy stuff he did, Augusto Pinochet continues to divide the people of Chile.

DID YOU KNOW?

- Although Pinochet portrayed himself as a populist and somewhat anti-intellectual, he amassed a library of more than 55,000 volumes.

- Pinochet married Luciana Hiriart in 1943. The couple had five children. Luciana and the Pinochet children were charged with embezzlement in the United States in 2007.

- In 2007, a Catholic priest named Luis Jorquera was charged with his involvement in the Caravan of Death. He was accused of working with death squad members to dig up the bodies of victims, putting them in helicopters, and then dumping them in the ocean.

- The paternal side of Pinochet's family is French-Bretton and his maternal side is Spanish and Basque.

- The bodies of death squad victims were usually placed in gunny sacks and then brought to Puma helicopters to be dumped in the ocean. Live victims were either severely beaten and/or drugged first to eliminate resistance.

IDI AMIN:

DID HE REALLY THINK HE WAS THE KING OF SCOTLAND?

As we continue our journey through the crazy things that dictators have done, it may sometimes seem like a descent into madness. Although there's really no way of knowing what another person is thinking, it's clear from the actions of some of these dictators that they had truly flipped their lids. Or that their lids were never on very tightly from the start.

That is the case of our next dictator—Idi Amin, otherwise known as the "Butcher of Uganda."

There's absolutely so much crazy sh*t Amin did that it could take up an entire book: from switching from pro-Western to pro-Soviet political sympathies to targeting his country's ethnic Indian population for persecution, there's no shortage of crazy policies Amin enacted that hurt his rule and his country. In the end, Amin's policies led to the deaths of up to 500,000 people in Uganda, and countless others were beaten, tortured, and raped.

But as truly awful as Amin's brutality was, even crazier were some of the other things he said and did while President of Uganda.

Amin actually claimed to be the "conqueror of the British Empire" and specifically the King of Scotland. He also gave himself an honorary law degree, although he never studied the law, and was always seen in public wearing aviator sunglasses and a military uniform festooned with medals.

The only problem was he never earned any of those medals.

Amin even considered erecting a statue of Adolf Hitler in the capital city of Kampala before he was driven out of power in 1979.

Idi Amin would be laughable if it weren't for the fact that he was responsible for so many deaths. Unlike many of the dictators in this book, Amin was said to have personally taken part in torture sessions and relished the activities.

The Army Cook

Idi Amin was not exceptional in any way. He wasn't good looking by Ugandan standards and he certainly wasn't an intellectual or even what most people would consider intelligent. He was, though, very lucky, and luck is often enough to win the day.

Idi Amin was born Idi Amin Dada Oumee, probably in 1925, in the Protectorate of Uganda, which was part of the British Empire. Little is known about his early life other than that he joined the British Colonial Army as a cook, where through the luck of history, he was able to advance quickly in the ranks.

When Uganda achieved independence in 1962, the army was in desperate need of men with military backgrounds, so Amin filled the void and was made an officer.

Despite his otherwise less than stellar qualities, Amin did have some athletic talent and he proved to be an excellent networker. He made connections with several important people, from different tribes and ethnic groups across Uganda who he would use when the military removed the president through a coup d'état in 1971.

The world soon found out just how crazy a dictator can be!

Uganda's Descent into Insanity

As soon as Amin was proclaimed president, it became painfully obvious to everyone that he was a special kind of crazy. He staffed the most important government and military positions with people from his Kakwa ethnic group, South Sudanese, whom he saw as loyal, and mercenaries from other parts of Africa.

Admin then earned his nickname "The Machete."

He persecuted ethnic groups that didn't support him, reserving special vitriol for the nation's 60,000 people of Indian and Pakistani descent. Amin argued that since many of those people were dual passport holders, they could not be trusted, so they were stripped of their property and "asked" to leave the country. As they did, many of the women were brutally raped by soldiers.

By 1972, Amin's instability was on full display for the world, which caused the United Kingdom, the United States, and several other Western powers to withdraw their support from the dictator. But doing so only pushed Amin into the Soviet sphere of influence and seemed to make him act even more erratic.

It was after 1972 that he began making the crazy claims about being the King of Scotland and winning all sorts of medals. It was also then that his brutality reached a new level, as he targeted both political *and* personal opponents.

The large and boisterous Amin always had a smile on his face, even—or especially—when others were suffering. He had the Bishop of the Anglican Church in Uganda assassinated and left on the side of a road for all to see.

And the warning was well-received by many.

But Amin's insanity and paranoia continued to grow and as it did he became more erratic and crueler.

He was said to enjoy killing his own government ministers by feeding them to the crocodiles in Lake Victoria.

Then there were the accusations of cannibalism. Amin was said to have used his culinary skills from the military to prepare dishes made from the flesh of his enemies. When *New York Times* reporter Ricardo Orizio asked Amin about the cannibalism accusations, he replied, "I don't like human flesh. It's too salty for me."

After starting an ill-fated war with neighboring Tanzania, Amin was forced to flee in exile on April 11, 1979. He died in Saudi Arabia on August 16, 2003, at the age of 78.

Idi Amin is remembered today as one of the most brutal and craziest dictators of the 20th century.

DID YOU KNOW?

- Amin had at least six wives and was married to three concurrently. Two of his former wives died under suspicious circumstances, with one being dismembered, and the whereabouts of a third remains unknown.

- PLO leader Yasser Arafat was the best man at Amin's wedding to Sarah Kyolaba in 1975. Her former boyfriend fled to Kenya and later disappeared.

- Amin had more than 50 children!

- Another bizarre thing that Amin was said to have done was to have white businessmen in Uganda carry him in his chair as if it were a palanquin.

- Idi Amin has been played by several different actors, including Forest Whitaker in *The Last King of Scotland* (2006), which won the American actor an Oscar.

JOSEPH STALIN:

FARMERS BAD, STARVATION GOOD

Dictators for the most part are very manipulative people. They know how to give the people what they want, when to take it from them, and what their weaknesses are.

The number one strength, or weakness, of any country, is its food supply and the people who produce that food. We've already seen how Pol Pot made the crazy decision of depopulating Cambodia's cities to punish his enemies. It led to widespread starvation, disease, and the ultimate downfall of the Khmer Rouge.

You'll see that starvation and using the food supply as a weapon is a reoccurring theme with our dictators.

Like, Pol Pot, Soviet dictator Joseph Stalin also attempted to weaponize his country's food supply, but he had fundamentally different reasons to do so. Although both dictators were communists, Pot saw the peasants as ideal socialists, while Stalin saw them as the enemy.

To Stalin, the peasants and small landowners, known in Russian as *kulaks*, were the enemy. The backbone of his new communist state, the United Soviet Socialist Republics (USSR), was the factory workers, while the kulaks represented monarchy, imperialism, conservatism, and the old ways.

So, to Stalin, the kulaks had to be eliminated.

Beginning in 1932, Stalin embarked on an ambitious program to strip the kulaks of their property and turn the farms, especially the breadbasket of Ukraine, into state-owned "collective" operations.

The result was one of the worst human rights catastrophes of the 20th century. Between four and 16 million people; mainly Ukrainians, died of starvation and disease in 1932 and 1933 in what became known as the *Holodomor* or Ukrainian genocide.

The Holodomor may have eliminated an entire class of Stalin's enemies, but it destroyed the Soviet Union's economy, killed many military-age men, and demoralized the country.

The result was the Soviet Union losing early battles in World War II and almost losing the war.

Steel Sounds Better

When Ioseb Besarionis dze Jugashvili entered the world on December 18, 1878, in the town of Gori, Georgia (the central Asian country, not the state in the American south), few thought that he'd make it big someday nor that he'd be responsible for as many as 20 million deaths.

The boy who would later become Stalin studied in a seminary for a while, but after determining that he was an atheist, he moved to Russia and became active in Marxist and communist circles.

By the early 1900s, Jugashvili earned quite a reputation as a man who wasn't afraid to get his hands dirty. He changed his name to the Russian "Joseph Stalin," with the last name meaning "steel."

Not only did the name sound more Russian, but it also was a clear statement about the man he wanted to become, and what he was becoming.

Stalin spent time in jail for a variety of crimes, many violent, which he did on behalf of the Bolshevik faction of the Russian communists. Stalin beat people up, committed robberies, and did vandalism and arson to forward his cause.

He learned that violence, fear, and terror could be very effective political tools when used properly.

When the Bolsheviks came to power in 1918 and when the Russian Communist Party was triumphant after the Russian Civil War in 1922, Stalin was there with Vladimir Lenin. Most members of the Communist Party didn't want to see Stalin anywhere near the levers of power, but when Lenin died in 1924, their worst nightmares came true.

And just as they thought, Stalin quickly began purging his enemies, real and perceived, from the Communist Party, the military, and eventually the farmers.

Stalin had a bone to pick with the farmers and he was going to make them starve to see his point.

The Holodomor

Whether Stalin targeted all Ukrainians as a form of punishment with the collectivization program is a subject of scholarly debate, but nearly all agree that his policies led to the Holodomor, which is a Ukrainian word for "death by hunger."

As the people of Ukraine starved since it was the most agriculturally productive part of the USSR, so too did the rest of the Soviet Union. The workers in the cities were provided with rations for a while, but they began disappearing and in their place was plenty of anti-kulak and anti-Ukrainian propaganda, in films, radio, and posters. Once the Holodomor ended and the bodies of the dead were disposed of, though, its long-term effects began to show.

After invading eastern Poland in September 1939, the Red Army attempted to follow that up with an invasion of Finland in November but could only achieve a Pyrrhic victory at best. In addition to purging some of the Red Army's best commanders, Stalin's forced collectivization left the rank-and-file with inadequate numbers.

By the time the Germans invaded the Soviet Union in 1941, the Red Army was a shadow of what it could have been, and when the Germans came plowing into Ukraine, they found many Ukrainians willing to help them. It wasn't that the Ukrainians were pro-German or pro-Nazi necessarily; they were anti-Russian and anti-Soviet due to the Holodomor.

Of course, Stalin and the Red Army went on to defeat Germany on the Eastern Front, but it was touch and go. Thanks to the crazy decision to starve the kulaks of Ukraine, the Soviets lost many more people than they needed to and nearly lost the war.

Not to mention, there are still major tensions between Ukraine and Russia today, much of it due to the crazy sh*t Stalin did while he was in power.

DID YOU KNOW?

- Because the Soviet Union was such a closed society, news of the Holodomor didn't reach the West until after World War II, when refugees from Eastern Europe brought the horror stories of their experiences with them.

- There is debate over whether the Holodomor specifically targeted the Ukrainian people and some debate whether it should be classified as "genocide." However, there is no debate that it happened.

- Russian leaders in the post-Soviet period admit that mass starvation took place in 1932-1933 in Ukraine, but refuse to consider it 'a genocide', stating that the Ukrainian people were not specifically targeted.

- After World War II, Stalin actually increased repression by opening a chain of *gulags* (prison camps) in Siberia and by deporting Baltic peoples from their homelands and spreading them out across the USSR.

- Joseph Stalin died on March 5, 1953, at the age of 73 from a cerebral hemorrhage in his dacha (cabin) outside Moscow.

NICOLAE CEAUŞESCU:

DO AS I SAY, NOT AS I DO

When Romanian dictator Nicolae Ceauşescu was overthrown on December 21, 1989, and executed the next day, it happened so quickly that many people around the world almost missed it. After all, it happened within the bigger picture of communism collapsing throughout Eastern Europe, so it was quickly overlooked in the chaos.

But Ceauşescu held the distinction of being only one of two of those governments to fall violently (we'll get to the other one,

Yugoslavia, a little later). The rest did so relatively peacefully. After the smoke in Romania cleared, though, the rest of the world began to see that Ceaușescu had enacted some truly repressive and crazy policies.

Like many other communist despots, including the two we've already profiled in our book, Ceaușescu limited his people's food rations, controlled the information they received, and even micromanaged the temperatures in their homes. But none of that was necessarily crazy. Ceaușescu never caused a massive famine in Romania and he is generally considered responsible for thousands, not millions of deaths.

The crazy thing that Ceaușescu did was believe his own hype. In 1971, after visiting communist North Korea, Ceaușescu decided to model his rule on dictators in that part of the world by carefully constructing his own "personality cult."

Perhaps to overcompensate for his diminutive stature (approximately 5ft 6 inches tall), Ceaușescu built himself and his wife up as the benevolent leaders of a socialist utopia, but socialism was a one-way street for him.

As the Romanian people struggled with food and energy rations during the 1970s and '80s, Ceaușescu and his family lived a capitalist lifestyle. In addition to a large presidential palace in Bucharest where they spent most of their time, the Ceaușescus had several country villas, lake cabins, and apartments throughout Romania. Ceaușescu enjoyed hunting, fishing, and entertaining world leaders at his many properties, sharing the finest Romanian wines with them, and dining on multi-course meals.

When communist regimes began collapsing in the late 1980s, Ceauşescu tried to hold things together through a combination of brutality and lies, but by then the people had seen through their leader's crazy policies and realized he was a hypocrite who had to go.

The Ashes of World War II

Nicolae Ceauşescu came of age during World War II in Romania, which was actually one of the Axis Powers and had a quasi-fascist government through most of the war. When the war began in 1939, Ceauşescu was a 21-year-old communist who thought he was going to change the world, but who found himself in concentration camps for most of the war.

Despite the hardships the future dictator endured, it wasn't all bad. He met his future wife, Elena, during the war and made important contacts that helped in later years.

When the Red Army occupied Romania after the war, Ceauşescu established himself a bona fide pro-Soviet, pro-Stalin communist. His ascent in the government was meteoric after that.

Ceauşescu became the General Secretary of the Romanian Communist Party in 1965, which was essentially the highest position in the land, and would later make himself president. The first few years of his rule were actually important and a bit unique compared to other Eastern Bloc countries.

Although Romania was a Warsaw Pact member, it differed in many international policies from its communist allies.

Ceauşescu recognized West Germany before other communist states did and recognized both Israel and the Palestine Liberation Organization as well. He was actually popular in Romania during the first few years of his rule, but then he visited North Korea and China in 1971 and everything changed.

When Ceauşescu returned from his Asian trip, he announced in his "July Thesis" that Romania would undergo a transformation just as China had (we'll get to that later in our book). Art would be changed, restrictions on travel were enacted, and most importantly, a massive propaganda campaign was initiated that stressed the primacy of Ceauşescu and his wife.

A Communist Living the Good Life

There were several problems with Ceauşescu assuming complete control of Romania. First, he was quite uneducated. With only a grade school equivalent education, Ceauşescu didn't have the background to deal with some of the complicated issues in front of him. Although there are plenty of intelligent people in the world who aren't very educated, he wasn't one of them.

Second, instead of accepting a confidant who was educated and/or intelligent, he chose his wife to be his right-hand person. Elena may have been charming, as Nicolae was, but like him, she wasn't too bright. Neither of the pair was very well-read nor well-spoken, but that didn't stop Nicolae from "awarding" his wife a Ph.D. in chemistry.

That was just the beginning of the ride on the crazy train for Ceauşescu and also marked the beginning of the end for him. To build his communist utopia, Ceauşescu had to borrow large amounts of foreign currency, and to pay that off, he had to enact strict austerity measures.

Fines or jail time were given for heating homes and offices above 60°F, curfews were common, and television consisted primarily of the "the leader" giving speeches with his wife standing next to him.

But the craziest things Ceauşescu did were related to food (there's that thing with food and dictators again). In 1982, the government announced a vigorous plan to combat obesity — although it really had more to do with paying back Romania's debts. The plan included lowering caloric intake to 2700-2800 calories a day. They did this by limiting pay and rations and by creating strange "mystery meat" food substitutes.

There was even a coffee called *nechezol* that was only 20% coffee and 80% chickpeas and beans!

Needless to say, chocolate, real coffee, cigars, and imported cigarettes, and even Soviet imports such as caviar, were considered luxury goods and off-limits to most people.They weren't off-limits to Ceauşescu and his family, though.

As the Romanian people struggled to pay back the loans their leader took out, Ceauşescu and his family lived the high life in their villas and mansions. Because Nicolae had complete control of the media, he was able to keep his lifestyle a secret for many years. He also used his secret police to arrest, torture, and imprison any dissenters.

But Ceauşescu's crazy policies and lifestyle couldn't be hidden forever. By the late 1980s, brave Romanians were beginning to protest about "the Leader" and it all came to a head on December 17, 1989, in the city of Timisoara. Thousands came out on that day to protest the dictator, but they were greeted with live ammunition from the police and military, leaving more than 100 dead.

Once Ceauşescu was executed, the people of Romania finally saw just how high on the hog the dictator lived and just how crazy he was.

DID YOU KNOW?

- Nicolae actually "stole" Elena away from one of his brothers. The couple married in 1939, had three children and remained married until they were executed in 1989.

- Ceauşescu developed a strange sort of friendship with Spanish artist Salvador Dali. The two men corresponded via letters and met in person in 1974 when the artist gave the dictator a scepter. Ceauşescu was said to have enjoyed the gift, although many contend that Dali meant it as a sarcastic joke. The joke was clearly over the dictator's head.

- Ceauşescu's height has been subject to debate. Some sources list him at a minuscule 5'2, while others have him at a more average 5'6.

- Romania under Ceauşescu was often a place with seemingly contradictory ideas, just as the dictator lived his life. For example, abortions were made illegal in 1966, but so too was going to church.

- Just months before he was removed from power and executed, Ceauşescu managed to repay the more than $11 billion in loans Romania owed.

NAPOLEON BONAPARTE:

RUSSIA WILL BE
EASY TO CONQUER

When you think of dictators, Napoleon Bonaparte usually isn't the first person to come to mind. He never subjected any people to mass starvation, he never devised a large and elaborate system of prison camps, and he never had pictures of himself painted and distributed throughout the land. Napoleon also didn't wear military medals that he didn't earn.

But make no mistake - Napoleon was a true dictator in every sense of the word.

Napoleon was a successful military general who came to power during the chaos of the French Revolution (1789-1799). As the smoke cleared, the French people wanted a strong leader, so who better to guide them than modern France's most successful military hero.

Although popular, Napoleon rigged the election to become consul (ruler) of France and he toppled one European monarch after another on his way to build the largest continental empire in modern history. Napoleon's dictatorial tendencies started to come out. He massacred resisters in various parts of Europe, especially Italy, and he began to see himself as something greater than he was.

Napoleon had himself crowned Emperor of France on December 2, 1804, in grand fashion, complete with a crown, specter, and throne. But as Napoleon became more and more powerful, the power went to his head. On June 24, 1812, Napoleon led his "Grand Army" of nearly 700,000 men east into Russia. Napoleon didn't intend to conquer Russia necessarily, but wanted to keep them from cooperating with the British, who were the primary enemy of the French.

Once again, it was the case where a dictator's hubris led him to make a crazy decision. Napoleon had every right to think that he would easily beat the Russians: his army was larger and better equipped, and most importantly, he was the best strategist in the world.

But Napoleon apparently wasn't much of a historian because if he were, he would have known about Charles XII of Sweden's attempted invasion of Russia in 1708-1709. It was crazy when Charles attempted it and Napoleon would find out that it was still crazy in 1812.

And it proved to be his undoing.

The Corsican Artillery Officer

When you think of France, you think of the Eiffel Tower, crepes, wine, and Napoleon, right? Well, the truth is that Napoleon was an ethnic Corsican and wasn't even born with French citizenship.

Napoleon was born on August 15, 1769, on the Mediterranean island of Corsica, which was ruled by the Italian city-state of Genoa at the time. Corsica was always more Italian than French, but in 1768 it was conquered by France.

So Napoleon had to become French.

Becoming French wasn't always easy for the Corsican mamma's boy, but he learned French and entered French military school when he was a teenager.

And a true star was born!

Napoleon was sharp and charismatic and by the time he graduated in 1785, he was an artillery lieutenant. In normal times he may have progressed slowly through the ranks—or not any further at all, considering that he wasn't part of the nobility—but destiny, fate, or luck, whichever one you believe, smiled on Napoleon when the French Revolution began.

As astute as the "little general" was with military tactics, he was equally capable in the political arena. When the revolution broke out, he saw that the momentum was with the revolutionaries and he also knew that if they came to power he would have a better chance of advancing.

So he chose to fight for the revolutionaries.

After winning the day for the revolutionaries at the Battle of Toulon in 1793 and getting wounded in the process, Napoleon was promoted to General at the tender age of 24. Not since Alexander the Great had such a young man taken the world by storm. And he was far from done.

After toppling most of the major monarchies of Western Europe, Napoleon defeated Russia and Austria at the Battle of Austerlitz on December 2, 1805, which ended the Holy Roman Empire and made him the sole ruler of continental Europe...pretty much.

Yes, Britain was over there on its island and Russia was off in the east somewhere.

Let's Go East Boys

So we come back to another one of our common themes with dictators—they begin believing their own hype; and since they're surrounded by sycophants, they do some pretty crazy sh*t that costs a lot of lives or collapses their governments.

In Napoleon's case, the sycophants were military men like him so they wanted to keep fighting, although by 1812, the French were facing setbacks in Spain. When the Russians declared their support for Britain and that they didn't want to be part of Napoleon's "continental system," the Corsican general decided it was a time to teach the Slavs a lesson.

It's not entirely fair to say that Napoleon didn't read history because he actually did study Charles XII's failed campaign, which is why he decided to invade in the summer. But it became immediately clear that he had failed to grasp just how vast Russia is, the swampy nature of its terrain, or the tenacity of the Russian people.

The Grand Army marched deeper and deeper into Russia, yet the Russians rarely engaged them with any significant numbers. It was almost as if they were drawing Napoleon in farther. Napoleon should have recognized that they were, but his pride got the better of him.

Finally, on September 7, the Grand Army arrived outside Moscow, but the Russians were waiting with a large force. The fighting was intense, but Napoleon won the day and the city. However, after moving the Grand Army into Moscow a week later, Napoleon soon realized he hadn't really won anything.

The city was largely abandoned, and worse, the Grand Army's supply lines were far overextended. They had survived by foraging, hunting, and looting, but as winter approached, there was far less to take.

So they began the long march back to friendly territory in Poland.

The Russian forces undertook numerous ambush attacks on the Grand Army as it retreated, which reduced its number and morale. Then, winter came early, and with no other choice, the soldiers had to eat all the horses.

The Russians wisely made deals with the Germans in the Grand Army to allow them safe passage, which reduced the army even more. Finally, the French found themselves eating their coats, boots, and whatever else they could find. The pains of hunger drove many of them to die of exposure.

More than half of the Grand Army died in the crazy expedition, more than 100,000 were captured, and nearly another 100,000 deserted.

As for Napoleon, his decision to invade Russia proved to be his true Waterloo.

His empire disintegrated and the French people turned on him, deposing him and then exiling him to the Mediterranean island of Elba. He later escaped Elba and had a brief return to rule, but he was quickly defeated and exiled for good to the Atlantic island of Saint Helena.

All because Napoleon made the crazy decision to invade Russia.

DID YOU KNOW?

- When one "meets his Waterloo," it means that that person has met his demise or failed in some way. It comes from Napoleon's final defeat at the Battle of Waterloo on June 18, 1815, although his true Waterloo was the failed invasion of Russia.

- Charles XII faced similar odds when he invaded Russia 100 years earlier, although the armies were much smaller. Charles actually began his invasion in the winter, which may have helped him when he got farther inland. The Russians, though, deployed the familiar tactic of hit-and-run attacks and retreating into the interior. Again, apparently Napoleon didn't study Charles XII enough.

- Napoleon was married twice and had one *legitimate* child with his second wife, Marie Louise the Duchess of Parma. Their son, Napoleon II, died of pneumonia at the age of 21 in 1832.

- Alexander I (reigned 1801-1825) was the Tsar of Russia at the time of Napoleon's invasion.

- Napoleon died on May 5, 1821, on the isolated British territory of Saint Helena at the age of 51. The cause of his death remains a mystery, with some believing he died of cancer while more conspiratorially-minded people think he was poisoned.

- Note: In 2007, American, Swiss and Canadian researchers applied modern pathological and tumor-staging methods to historical accounts and found that Napoleon died of a very advanced case of gastric cancer that stemmed from an ulcer-causing bacterial infection in his stomach, rather than a heretofore belief of a hereditary disposition to the cancer. The analysis, which also refutes rumors of arsenic poisoning, points to gastrointestinal bleeding as the likely immediate cause of death.

KIM JONG-IL:

DEAR LEADER, WE
NEED SOME FOOD

The 1990s may have seemed like a boring time for many people in the world, especially historians. When the Cold War ended in 1991 with the dissolution of the Soviet Union, most people around the world breathed a sigh of relief, as it was believed that the threat of nuclear Armageddon had dissipated. It also seemed that Western ideas of democracy and capitalism had won, leading writer Francis Fukuyama to declare "The End of History."

As much as Fukuyama's thesis may have been intriguing, it simply wasn't true. It also wasn't true that nothing happened in the world after 1991, as all of you reading this know very well. The concept of communism persisted, in some form, in places such as China, Cuba, and North Korea, and it was in North Korea where some of the more interesting—and brutal—post-Cold War incidents took place.

In the 1990s, North Korea was ruled by a man named Kim Jong-Il, who ran his country with brutal efficiency, employing a blend of a Marxist-communist-Soviet style government and system founded on ancient Asian concepts of warlord dynasties. He inherited the rulership of North Korea gradually from his father, Kim Il-Sung, until he died in 1994, which gave Jong-Il complete control of the country and the ability to implement all his ideas.

Many of Kim Jong-Il's policies were in keeping with those of his predecessors, although he obviously also did some crazy things if he's on our list here, right? Well, as Kim Jong-Il gained more and more power in North Korea, like his father, and like all of the dictators in this book, he developed a personality cult. He became known as "Dear Leader." The Dear Leader was faced with many problems after his father died and he dealt with them in the craziest sort of way.

The dissolution of the Soviet Union created economic problems and food shortages in North Korea, but instead of dealing with the situation directly, Jong-Il decided to double down on the policy of *Songun*, a military-first government policy. The result was a famine that lasted from 1994 to 1998, killing between a quarter of a million and 3.5 million people. We may never know the true extent of the North Korean famine due to the nature of the North Korean government, but we do know that it was devastating.

Besides the immense amount of human suffering and death the famine caused, it also further isolated North Korea from the rest of the world.

Like Father, Like Son

When Kim Jong-Il became the leader of communist North Korea, known officially as the "Democratic People's Republic of Korea," he instituted a repressive, authoritarian regime that borrowed heavily from communist ideology and traditional elements of Korean culture. Il-Sung (his father) had cozied up to both China and the Soviet Union, which he needed to do to survive the Korean War, but also to promote the idea of him as the "father" of the North Korea people. Il-Sung drew the concept of the "Father" heavily from Confucianism and ancient Korean ancestor worship.

But make no mistake, Il-Sung was no Ward Cleaver-type father.

Dissenters were regularly punished by being sent to labor camps where they worked on public works projects, often until death. Additionally, to top things off, if the dissenters were a real pain in the butt, then his or her whole family would be sent to the camp with them!

As repressive as the system was, it was orderly and the constant threat of "imperialist" invasions by the "Yankees" and their Korean lackeys in South Korea (disseminated through propaganda messages) kept the people of North Korea in a heightened sense of panic. So if the crops didn't produce as much as they should, the Soviet Union or China was always there to bail North Korea out.

But once the Soviet Union collapsed, the old North Korean Songun military system became a whole lot less practical.

Kim Jong-Il was designated his father's successor in 1974, so you'd think he would have learned the nuances of running a dictatorship, but the collapse of the Soviet Union left him without extra resources. A more far-sighted leader would've realized that the military threat from the United States was minimal and that he could've diverted some resources from the military to food production.

But instead, Kim Jong-Il made the crazy decision of keeping the Songun at its Cold War levels.

Bombs Not Food

There is little doubt that the North Korean Famine could've been avoided, or at least mitigated to a major extent, if Kim Jong-Il didn't keep the disastrous policies of his father. With that said, there are major topographical and climatic differences between North Korea and South Korea that made the famine worse.

North Korea is colder and more mountainous than South Korea, which means that cultivatable land is in short supply and the growing seasons are much shorter. There were also floods and drought in the mid-1990s that exacerbated the situation, but for the most part, the famine was human-made.

As the returns on the crops began to diminish, Jong-Il allocated most of the food to the military, leaving the rest of North Korea's 22 million people to live on meager rations.

If you were a good little communist worker, you were given 900 grams a day of food, but if you were just a non-party worker, you only got 700 grams. Grandma and grandpa suffered the most, with retired workers only getting 300 grams of food per day.

And the food the people received, which consisted primarily of rice and corn, had very little nutritional value.

Starvation became rampant, especially in the cities, and with the starvation came a host of diseases, including dysentery. Although the peasants didn't suffer quite as much as the townsfolk, as they were able to grow some of their own food, the famine brought devastation to all quarters of North Korea.

So anyone who dared notice what was happening ran the risk of being sent to a prison camp. Still, the people did notice and—in private—fingers were being pointed at the Dear Leader.

So just like any other capable despot, Kim Jong-Il found a scapegoat.

Kwan-hui, the North Korean minister of agriculture, was accused of spying for the United States and for causing the famine. He was tried and convicted in a show trial and publicly executed by firing squad in 1997.

The North Korean Famine eventually subsided after the international community donated tons of food, but as we'll see later, the repression and crazy stuff continue today.

DID YOU KNOW?

- Kim Jong-Il tried to portray the famine in revolutionary terms as a fight that he called the "Arduous March" or the "March of Suffering." He compared it to the fight in which his father engaged the Japanese during World War II.

- North Korea became a nuclear power under Kim Jong-Il. Despite signing an agreement with the United States in 1994 to dismantle their nuclear weapons program, just as the famine was beginning, they continued to build anyway.

- Kim Jong-Il was born in 1941, although the precise date and place of his birth are a matter of debate. Korea was occupied by Japan at the time, so many of the records for that period were lost.

- Like most dictators, Kim Jong-Il carefully crafted his public image by always wearing plain, peasant clothes, but he supposedly had more the $4 billion stashed in different European banks.

- Kim Jong-Il died on December 17, 2011, of a heart attack at the age of 70 in the capital city of Pyongyang. The torch was then passed to his son, Kim Jong-Un who is the current leader of North Korea.

RAFAEL TRUJILLO:

"GOD IN HEAVEN,
TRUJILLO ON EARTH"

When we think of a prototypical Latin American dictator, leftwing or rightwing, images of a man with carefully coifed facial hair wearing a uniform with plenty of medals and possibly a nice pair of aviator sunglasses come to mind. Pinochet, who we've already met, and Castro, who we'll meet later, more or less conformed to that image.

But the originator of that image, the archetype if you will, was

Dominican Republic dictator President Rafael Trujillo, otherwise known as "El Jefe," or "the Boss."

In addition to being the first true modern Latin American dictator, Trujillo was one of the longest-serving dictators on our list, ruling the Dominican Republic from 1930 until he was assassinated in 1961. During that long rule, Trujillo tortured and killed thousands of his countrymen, engaged in a campaign of ethnic cleansing against Haitians that many consider genocide, and even had many of his enemies assassinated in foreign countries.

And in true dictator fashion, Trujillo developed a cult of personality through in-depth propaganda, which included monuments of El Jefe scattered throughout the Dominican Republic and films that portrayed him as a benevolent leader. He was even credited with coining the slogan: "God in Heaven, Trujillo on Earth."

In Trujillo's case, it wasn't just one crazy thing that led to his demise but really a whole series of events and actions. Trujillo was a man who believed in living by the sword and it was that crazy belief that ended with him dying by the sword.

A Ph.D. in Thuggery

Trujillo was born Rafael Leonidas Trujillo Molina (these names are ordered according to Latin American naming tradition) on October 24, 1891, in San Cristobal, Dominican Republic to Jose and Silveria Trujillo. He was raised in a middle-class family but became involved in criminal activity at a young age. Young Rafael wasn't afraid to mix it up in fights with older kids and adults and thought nothing of stealing or robbing from people at knifepoint.

Rafael worked his way up quickly in the local criminal hierarchy, although his recognition on the streets also brought him to the attention of local law enforcement, landing him in prison for several months.

By the time Trujillo was in his mid-twenties, he looked like just another throw-away Dominican kid. With no real marketable skills other than thuggery, it looked as though he'd probably have longer and longer stretches in prison to look forward to and more than likely an early death.

But then the Yankees came in 1916.

The Marines landed in the Dominican Republic that year to make the government pay debts it owed and to "restore order," which meant installing a pro-American government. To do that, the Americans had to establish a military that was tough yet compliant with their goals.

The Yankees were willing to train anyone, as long as the applicants weren't afraid to get their hands dirty.

Rafael Trujillo was cut out perfectly for the job!

After earning his Ph.D. in thuggery on the streets of the Dominican Republic, Trujillo applied those ideas and tactics to the new Dominican military, moving up quickly in the ranks. By 1930, he was the commander-in-chief of the entire Dominican armed forces and played a major role in the coup d'état that toppled the existing government.

Trujillo was "elected" president in an election in 1930 and re-elected in 1938. He was also president from 1942 to 1952, but between and after those terms, Trujillo was the true power in the Dominican Republic, and everyone knew it.

He organized many of the street gangs into pro-government paramilitary forces and he introduced the idea of death squads, which became much more common in Latin American in the 1970s and '80s. Trujillo ruled by decree and if any visible opposition to his rule cropped up, he had the offenders murdered, arrested, or "disappeared."

In 1937, he had between 20,000 to 30,000 ethnic Haitian civilians killed in a border conflict known the "Parsley Massacre."

When Castro and the communists came to power in nearby Cuba in 1959, another enemy was added to Trujillo's list.

By 1961, Trujillo had been doing crazy stuff for more than 30 years—violent repression, corruption, and amassing a mile-long enemies list—so it wasn't a shock to many when his roosters finally came home to roost.

Take a Number Please

When Rafael Trujillo was assassinated on May 30, 1961, not many people around the world were very surprised. The fact that he was shot to death in broad daylight as his motorcade drove through the capital city of Santo Domingo should have been jarring, to say the least. However, since Trujillo was such a lightning rod and made so many enemies, no one really flinched.

Perhaps that was the final crazy thing Trujillo did—being so careless with his security and not realizing that he had an especially long enemies list.

But it may not have mattered anyway.

It was immediately revealed that Trujillo's murder was part of a conspiracy by the upper ranks of the military, which was not so surprising, but it was also determined that the CIA played an active role as well. It seems that the CIA just got tired of Trujillo's crazy behavior and decided to do away with him and give the job to someone more to their liking.

DID YOU KNOW?

- Besides killing and imprisoning thousands, Trujillo also used his country's treasury as a personal piggy bank to make him and his family very wealthy.

- Trujillo publicly professed to be a Roman Catholic as part of his image, but he was married three times and had many mistresses, which he often flaunted in the open. El Jeffe also had at least seven children.

- Although the world knew well of Trujillo's brutality, the Dominican Republic joined the United Nations during his rule.

- In addition to helping Trujillo come to power, the American Marines also brought baseball to the Dominican Republic, which today is the country's most popular sport by far.

- Trujillo was said to carry a list of names of those he wanted killed throughout the world. He would offer high rewards to successful assassins.

MUAMAR GADDAFI:

WHY DIDN'T HE
PROMOTE HIMSELF?

Aviator sunglasses…check! Plenty of medals never won in battle…check! Female bodyguards…

Meet former Libyan dictator Muammar Gaddafi, known to his people as the "Brotherly Leader and Guide of the Revolution of Libya," or sometimes just as "Colonel Gaddafi." Gaddafi was perhaps the most eccentric dictator in our book; he did plenty of crazy stuff that had all kinds of repercussions on his rule, his country, and the world.

At first glance, Gaddafi looks like just a standard, tin-pot dictator, but a closer look reveals a man who truly lived in his own world.

Once referred to by American President Ronald Reagan as the "mad dog of the Middle East," Gaddafi was a high-profile dictator during the Cold War not only for his support of anti-Western governments and dissidents, and at times terrorists, but also for his eccentricities.

Although he ruled his country with an iron fist, he never promoted himself to General, which is certainly strange for a dictator. Gaddafi shared paranoia with the other dictators on our list, but he reacted to it in truly unique ways: he had a bulletproof tent, imported nurses from Ukraine, and was protected by an all-female staff of bodyguards.

And that's just some of the crazy that the Libyan dictator exuded daily.

The Poor Bedouin

Muammar Mohammed Abu Minyar al-Gaddafi was born into a poor Bedouin family in Libya during World War II. Although he was never a particularly religious person, Libya is an Islamic country and the educational system Gaddafi experienced was heavily infused with religion. Young Gaddafi accepted his religious background but was more influenced by the burgeoning Arab nationalism of the 1950s.

Gaddafi was impressed with Egypt's dictator, Gamal Nasser, and the stance he took on behalf of his people against the West. Nasser would play a major role in the ideology and style that Gaddafi would later adopt when he became ruler.

After getting arrested for taking part in a pro-Islamic demonstration that turned violent, Gaddafi joined the Libyan military and found his true calling.

Gaddafi initially had a difficult time adjusting to the regimentation of military life. It wasn't that he wasn't able to do the work or even that he disliked it, but he had problems with the British officers who staffed the army's ranks in the 1960s.

Despite his obstinacy, though, he advanced through the ranks and was even sent to an English immersion camp in England in 1966. By that time, Gaddafi had moved past his initial negative attitude toward the English, but his eccentricities were on full display.

When Gaddafi visited London, he did so wearing traditional Libyan garb. He raised more than a few eyebrows when he was there and his training officers were also amused. To them, Gaddafi was a good-hearted bloke, if not a little "off," who was for the most part harmless.

Little did they know.

The Revolutionary Nuns

In 1969, Gaddafi played a central role in the overthrow of Libya's king, Idris I. The coup left Gaddafi as head of state and, as his first act, he promoted himself from lieutenant to *colonel*. Yes, that's right, for whatever reason he just didn't go ahead and make himself general. It was truly indicative of Gaddafi's unpredictable nature.

The Colonel immediately made big and sometimes draconian changes to Libyan society. Christian churches were closed and alcohol was banned in the name of Islamic law. But at the same time, women were given more rights than they had under the previous monarchy.

He also expelled all the Jews and Italians from Libya.

In terms of foreign policy, Gaddafi adopted a very anti-Western stance that vacillated from Arab nationalism to Islamism, and then to Marxism. He claimed that he was anti-Marxist since Marxism was atheistic, but he developed close relations with the communist bloc and he instituted socialism in Libya. Gaddafi proclaimed Islam as the only religion of Libya, but he would persecute Islamic fundamentalists along with his political enemies. In his early years of rule, he cozied up to Arab nationalist regimes, such as Nasser's Egypt, but in the later years of his rule, he professed alliances and unity with sub-Saharan Africa.

Truly, Gaddafi was an enigma and appeared quite crazy to outsiders. His anti-Western ideology and theatrics led him to make Libya a safe haven for radical and terrorist groups, which resulted in an American air bombing mission on the country in 1986.

Gaddafi's crazy decisions about the friends he kept in the 1970s and '80s led to disastrous consequences, as his home was targeted in the 1986 bombing, possibly killing one of his daughters.

But just like we've seen throughout this book, tragedies and brushes with death only seem to drive most dictators to double down on the craziness.

By the late 1980s, Gaddafi's behavior was increasingly eccentric, or perhaps it was just noticed more.

He didn't go anywhere without his retinue of female bodyguards known as "The Revolutionary Nuns." When asked why his bodyguards were female, Gaddafi responded that Muslim assassins would hesitate to kill women.

Gaddafi also had a staff of Ukrainian nurses to care for him. The nurses were led by a buxom woman named Galyna Kolotnytska, who was said to care for the Colonel in a number of ways.

Good news came for Gaddafi in 2006 when the United States took Libya off its list of nations that sponsored terrorism. The move meant that Gaddafi could more freely travel around the world and even visit the United States, but he couldn't stand flying and could only fly for eight hours at a time, which meant that Gaddafi had to take circuitous routes to arrive at his locations.

In late 2010, it looked as though the eccentric Colonel had

reformed his crazy ways and was going to join the community of nations. He visited the United States to attend the United Nations General Assembly, and as strange and rambling as his speech there was, it was considered innocuous.

But then the Arab Spring happened.

The Arab Spring protest movement in Libya descended into a civil war, which ended when NATO airstrikes helped Gaddafi's enemies come to power. Once they got a hold of Gaddafi, there were apparently still plenty of people who were unhappy with his crazy ideas and actions in the previous decades, so they brutally and publicly executed him on October 20, 2011.

So ended the life of what was perhaps the most eccentric and craziest dictator of all.

DID YOU KNOW?

- Some of Gaddafi's female bodyguards later accused him of rape and torture.

- Gaddafi was accused of having his foreign secretary killed and then kept in a freezer so he could see the body.

- Perhaps owing to his Bedouin roots, Gaddafi hated heights and would only stay on the first floor of hotels. When he attended the United Nations General Assembly in 2010, he brought his bulletproof tent and camels and stayed in New Jersey.

- Gaddafi started a war with Chad in 1969 that left more than 7,000 of his people dead and a war with Egypt in 1977 that killed 400 Libyans. He is also often credited for hundreds or even thousands of deaths through terrorist proxies, but the number of domestic enemies he had tortured and killed remains unknown, although it is believed to at least be in the hundreds.

- Gaddafi had nine children, two adopted, with his second wife, Safia Farkash.

ROBERT MUGABE:

"LET ME BE A HITLER TENFOLD"

Our next dictator is an interesting case because he not only did some crazy things that caused a lot of misery, he was one of the few cases that had a lot of outside support and people who hoped he'd succeed. Robert Mugabe was the first leader of Zimbabwe, first as the prime minister from 1980 until 1987, and then as the president until he retired in 2017.

He was a member of the majority Shona ethnic group and a former guerilla fighter. Everyone knew that Mugabe was tough, but most hoped that he'd be willing to form a new, equitable nation in the ashes of the former white minority dominated Rhodesia.

Most were happy when he gave a speech shortly after taking office that seemed to indicate that he would be conciliatory toward the white minority:

"It could never be a correct justification that because the whites oppressed us yesterday when they had power, the blacks must oppress them today."

It didn't take long, though, for him to go back on his word.

Rhodesians/white Zimbabweans numbered about 250,000 when Mugabe came to power and within a decade their numbers were less than 100,000. Mugabe decided to give in to his hate and embarked on a crazy campaign to dispossess the whites of all their lands and businesses, which led to economic collapse, sending the once-prosperous African nation into despair.

But to be fair, Mugabe also targeted his black political rivals, members of the Ndebele ethnic group, and middle-class and wealthy blacks who supported the white-controlled Rhodesian government. By the time Mugabe died in 2017, he was responsible—directly and indirectly—for the deaths of thousands in his small country.

Mugabe's crazy antics all but destroyed his country and made it an international pariah.

Mugabe the Guerilla

Robert Gabriel Mugabe was born and raised in the British colony of Southern Rhodesia in southern Africa. Although raised in the Catholic Church, young Robert knew that religion wasn't for him, but in the traditional and tribal society that he lived in, he learned to keep his mouth shut. Robert respected his elders, but even more so he knew from a young age that there was a time and a place for every battle.

Mugabe's battle would be fought later with words *and* guns.

Mugabe was educated by Jesuits and taught at Jesuit schools for blacks throughout Southern Rhodesia. He then earned a spot at the University of Fort Hare in South Africa in 1949. Fort Hare was a black university that became a hotbed of revolutionary activism during the 1950s. Mugabe made contacts with the African National Congress (ANC) and became well-versed in Marxism. He then took those ideas and tactics with him back to Southern Rhodesia.

Similar to the situation in South Africa, Southern Rhodesia — and later Rhodesia — was ruled by a sizable white minority, although there were some notable differences between the two countries. South Africa was much larger in size and population than Rhodesia, which was still part of the British Empire until it declared its independence in 1965.

South Africa, conversely, was independent and its government was completely dominated by the white minority, which enacted rigid racial laws. Although Rhodesia was ruled by the white minority, it allowed some black representation in its government, and its racial laws were far looser.

Both countries, though, had growing black liberation and Marxist/communist movements in the 1960s.

Mugabe traveled throughout Africa in the late 1950s and early 1960s, refining his Marxist ideas and mixing them with the teachings of African nationalist Kwame Nkrumah.

The young Shona had become a well-known revolutionary theorist, so when he returned to Rhodesia in 1963, he was promptly put in prison until 1975.

Mugabe very well could've died in prison, but due to luck or fate, he was released. The Bush War (1964-1975) had been raging for years between Rhodesia and various black nationalist and Marxist groups, so Rhodesian Prime Minister Ian Smith was trying anything to keep his hold on power. He agreed to release a number of black revolutionaries as a sign of goodwill during the negotiations.

Robert Mugabe was one of those released.

At that point, Mugabe could've gone quietly away, or even moved to the safety of the West, or the communist bloc, and lived a life of luxury as a sought-after speaker. Instead, he chose to fight in the bush.

Well, he was more of an organizer and motivational speaker than an actual fighter, but he was in the bush at the camps with the fighters, and when Smith agreed to bring Rhodesia back into the British Empire in 1979, it meant that black rule was coming to Rhodesia.

The Weapon of Fear

Despite being afraid of their standing in society and for their lives, Mugabe reassured the white minority that he wouldn't target them.

And for the first few years of the 1980s that was true for the most part.

The large, wealthy farms that were owned and operated by whites were left alone and actually prospered, which was also good for rural blacks because they comprised most of the farm workforce.

Urban whites, though, faced a different reality. The legal segregation of neighborhoods ended, civil service jobs were increasingly given to blacks over whites, and other skilled jobs were also being won by blacks.

The urban whites left in droves for South Africa, the United Kingdom, Australia, Canada, and the United States, but the farmers hung on until the 1990s.

By 2000, Mugabe had been in power for 20 years and there were grumblings within the black community in Zimbabwe about his rule. He had all opposition members imprisoned, killed, or intimidated, but there were whispers within his own ZANU-Patriotic Front Party.

They said that the white farmers were too rich, had all the good land at black people's expense and that the war veterans should have a piece of the pie.

Mugabe reacted by officially ordering land appropriation, which took land from the white farmers and theoretically gave it to disadvantaged Zimbabweans. The reality is that most of the farms went to government officials who sold and gave them away in a spoils system.

The farms that weren't officially re-appropriated were taken by force while the government watched.

Of the more than 5,000 white-owned farms when the seizures began in 2000, less than 500 still exist.

Mugabe famously said during the seizures:

"You are now our enemies because you really have behaved as enemies of Zimbabwe. We are full of anger. Our entire community is angry and that is why we now have the war veterans seizing land."

It may have seemed like a good political move to Mugabe, but the farm seizures sent Zimbabwe's economy into a tailspin. Unemployment, hyperinflation, and food shortages all marked the country's decline until Mugabe's death. But as crazy as the farm seizures idea was, Mugabe didn't regret a thing.

"If that is Hitler, then let me be a Hitler tenfold," said Mugabe in 2003.

DID YOU KNOW?

- Mugabe was also not a fan of gay rights, saying in 2013: "Obama came to Africa saying Africa must allow gay marriages...God destroyed the Earth because of these sins. Marriage is between a man and a woman."

- Mugabe single-handedly revised Zimbabwe's constitution in 1987 to eliminate the office of the prime minister and make the president the primary executive.

- Although Zimbabwe is technically a democracy and there are opposition parties, Mugabe and the ZANU-PF managed to hold power through a combination ballot stuffing and rigging and voter intimidation.

- Mugabe was married twice and had four children. He had one child with his first wife, Sally, although that child died in 1966. The other three children he had with his second wife, Grace, who is 41 years younger than him.

- Robert Mugabe died on September 9, 2019, in a hospital in Singapore at the age of 95.

ADOLF HITLER:

THAT RUSSIA THING AGAIN

Let's go from the black Hitler to the real Hitler. Of course, Adolf Hitler needs no introduction in the world of dictators, as he stands above all others, except for maybe Stalin, in terms of brutality and a bad reputation. Hitler's body count has been put in the tens of millions if you consider World War II itself, along with the concentration camps and the others who died as he rose to power in the Nation Socialist German Workers' Party and later in the German government.

Hitler was known for his oratory skills and his fanatical hatred of the Jews, and he was full of many crazy ideas.

But what was the craziest thing Hitler did and why?

There are a lot of things that could fit this category, but from a purely objective, strategic perspective, Hitler's invasion of the Soviet Union, known as "Operation Barbarossa," was the craziest thing.

It was so crazy because from Hitler and Nazi Germany's perspective there was no need to do so. Hitler had just made peace with the USSR in the Nazi-Soviet Pact and Stalin showed no signs of wanting to attack Germany.

Sure, the two dictators were diametrically opposed politically, and their egos were bound to brush against each other sooner or later, but from 1939, when the two countries signed the pact, to 1941, when Operation Barbarossa took place, the Soviet Union was in no position to wage a protracted war against a capable enemy.

Do you remember reading about the Holodomor? That disaster effectively crippled Stalin's Red Army?

So, if the Soviet Union posed no threat to Hitler and Germany, why did the German dictator make the crazy decision of invading? After all, surely Hitler knew about Charles XII and Napoleon, right? Well, he did know about them but his visions of an Aryan utopia were just more important. You see, Hitler hated people of Slavic background almost as much as the Jews and he saw Eastern Europe, where the Slavs live, as the location for future colonization and part of his visionary "Greater Germanic Reich."

Hitler's brash decision to invade the Soviet Union turned all of Europe into a battlefield and was one of the major factors in the dictator's demise.

From Vienna to Berlin

Adolf Hitler's early life has been examined and re-examined by countless historians and psychologists, so I'll do you a favor and not add to the list here. Suffice to say, some of the ideas he learned in his youth shaped who he became later and played a role in his crazy decision to invade Russia.

Hitler was born in 1889 in what was known as at the time as the Austro-Hungarian Empire. The part he was born in is today the German-speaking and ethnically German Austria, but back then the country was a mix of many different European nationalities.

And Hitler didn't like it!

When he lived in Vienna as a student, he wrote that he grew to detest the Jewish and Slavic populations of the city and that he yearned to know what it was like to live in a true Germanic country.

So when World War I began in 1914, instead of fighting for his native-born Austria-Hungary, he volunteered to fight in the army of that country's ally, Germany.

Hitler's time in the trenches of World War I only seemed to

harden his resolve to build a German utopia and the experience also apparently gave him a newfound militancy.

After the war, as is the case with many modern war veterans, Hitler had a difficult time adjusting at first, but he eventually found his place in politics with the fledgling German Workers' Party, later to be renamed the National Socialist German Workers' Party or the Nazi Party for short.

When Hitler and his buddies failed to take over the German state of Bavaria in a 1923 putsch, he landed in prison for just over a year.

But the year gave Hitler time to write *Mein Kampf* and to reflect on the direction of his party. He rebranded the National Socialists, took advantage of current economic and social problems, and came to power in 1932.

Once Hitler and the Nazis were in power, they immediately began the program on which they had campaigned. The Jews were persecuted, communists and other political opponents were killed and put in concentration camps, and the entire country began mobilizing for war.

Hitler envisioned the Germanic countries of Norway, Denmark, Sweden, the Netherlands, and Belgium being part of his Germania—whether they wanted to or not, of course— and the Slavic lands east of Germany being ethnically cleansed for a colonizing population of Germanic peasants. The Baltic peoples would be "allowed' to stay, although they would eventually be "Germanized."

The USSR and Stalin stood in the way of Hitler's Germanic

utopia, so he had to make the crazy decision and became yet another leader who thought invading the giant country was a good idea.

Russia Will Be Easy to Conquer: Part II

Although most of Hitler's military high command didn't necessarily share his political and racial views, they knew that speaking out against him was bad for their health. But they were also career military men who loved a good war and knew that there could be some promise to invading the Soviet Union.

If they were able to capture the Caucus oil fields, they would have nearly unlimited fuel to fight the British, and possibly the Americans in the future.

So, the generals began plotting with Hitler how best to invade Russia.

When Germany invaded and conquered Poland in September 1939, the Soviet Red Army moved in on the eastern half of that country. Outwardly, it seemed as though the two dictators had come to an agreement, but make no mistake, they were diametrically opposed to each other. Stalin considered that Germany would invade, but he reasoned that he had more than enough men to deter any such thoughts.

We've already seen that Stalin had plenty of crazy ideas before the war, but by 1941, Hitler overtook him in the crazy department.

Planning for the invasion of the Soviet Union began in 1940 and, by the end of that year, it was codenamed "Operation Barbarossa" for the Holy Roman Emperor Fredrick I the "Red Beard" (1122-1190).

Hitler sure loved history and the glories of Germany's past, but if he were a true student of history, he would've studied Charles XII's and Napoleon's failed invasions of Russia. Hitler believed that the situation in 1941 was different, as Germany's technological superiority would allow them to win the war quickly.

So, on June 22, 1941, Hitler made perhaps the craziest decision of his life when he ordered the invasion of the Soviet Union. At first, things went well, with the combined Axis forces of Germany, Hungary, Romania, Italy, Finland, Croatia, and volunteers from Spain numbering close to four million men.

They attacked along a nearly 2,000-mile front, quickly moving into Russia and getting near their objectives within months.

But by December 1941, the Axis forces faced the same problems encountered by Charles XII and Napoleon: overextension of supply lines, difficult weather, the vastness of Russia, and an underestimated enemy resolve.

When the Axis were unable to capture their objectives in early 1942, they initiated a slow retreat back west. The Axis committed numerous atrocities on enemy soldiers and civilians alike, so the Red Army returned the favor. There were very few prisoners of war on the Eastern Front during World War II.

By the time Hitler met his final demise in his Berlin bunker on April 30, 1945, there were several crazy things he had done, but probably none stood out more than Operation Barbarossa.

In the end, though, there were plenty of people around the world who were glad that Hitler made that crazy move because it was ultimately what brought down his regime.

DID YOU KNOW?

- The Axis Powers suffered more than one million casualties during Operation Barbarossa. The Romanian Army was all but destroyed and the other smaller Axis Powers began changing sides as soon as the Axis retreat began.

- Besides having the element of surprise and being better equipped, the early Axis victories in Barbarossa were partly the result of some other crazy sh*t Stalin did. Remember how he sent thousands to the prisons known as gulags? Well, many of the old-school officers from the Imperial Russian Army were among those executed or sent to the prisons, generally referred to as "purged," so the leadership of the Red Army was initially weak and "green" in World War II.

- Thankfully for Stalin, General Georgy Zhukov was not purged. Zhukov was one of the best overall generals in World War II and is considered to be the savior of the Soviet Union.

- Operation Barbarossa was originally planned to commence in May, but for reasons unknown, it was delayed for over a month. Whether that extra month would've given the Axis forces victory is a source of debate.

- Walther von Brauchitsch was the commander-in-chief

of the German military during Barbarossa. He was blamed for its failure and dismissed from service, although he was allowed to live!

SADDAM HUSSEIN:

LETTING THE KIDS RUN WILD

Since he is a pretty recent dictator, we tend to know more about former Iraqi President Saddam Hussein than most of the others on our list. We know him as the guy who invaded Kuwait in 1990 and who then had his country invaded by an American-led military coalition in 1991.

The Americans returned again in 2003, toppled his government, arrested him while he was on the run, and handed him over to his enemies who executed him on December 30, 2006.

Before his execution, though, Saddam Hussein left a large swath of misery across the Middle East. He invaded Iranian territory in 1980, setting off the Iran-Iraq War, which left more than one million people dead. As crazy as that was, though, there were plenty of other crazy things he did while in power.

He was the only national leader to use chemical weapons since the world wars, he routinely imprisoned, tortured, and murdered his political opponents, and he waged a war of repression and discrimination against the largest religious group in his country, the Shiite Muslims.

But perhaps the crazy thing he did that had some pretty horrific consequences was letting his two sons, Qusay and Uday, do whatever they wanted.

Perhaps, it wasn't all their fault, as Saddam was said to have brought them to watch torture sessions and executions when they were children. Still, the two young men subjected Iraq to a special kind of terror and maliciousness that even their father didn't seem to possess. He put Uday and Qusay in positions of power and, in return, they helped bankrupt the nation and committed acts of violence and rape against innocent Iraqis with impunity.

Qusay and Uday were a major reason why so many Iraqis turned against their once populist leader.

Raised by Wolves

Saddam Hussein was born in 1937 in the northern Iraqi town of Tikrit. It was truly a different era: Iraq was still part of the British Empire and World War II was still a couple of years away. Saddam's father died before he was born and his mother didn't want him, so he was raised by his uncle Talfah.

Talfah was perhaps the greatest influence in the future dictator's life. He was the father of Saddam's first wife (yes, Saddam married his first cousin!) and he imbued in his protégé many of the ideas and activities for which Saddam was later known. Talfah was an ardent Arab nationalist and he was also a bit of a crook. Saddam later combined those ideas when he came to power.

Things actually could've gone much differently for Hussein. He was a school teacher for several years and, by all accounts, was good at it, but his political activities were more important to him.

Saddam Hussein crossed the Rubicon when he became involved in a plot to assassinate the leader of Iraq in 1959. Although the plot was unsuccessful and forced Saddam into years of exile in Syria and Egypt, it gained him an immense amount of respect from his fellow Ba'ath Party members. He then served a couple of years in Iraqi prison during the 1960s for political crimes and, by that time, he was firmly entrenched in the inner workings of the Ba'ath Party.

And he knew that, in the cutthroat world of Iraqi politics, violence was *always* the answer.

After the Ba'ath Party assumed power of Iraq in 1968, Saddam became head of the armed forces and the police, which he used to ruthlessly suppress all political discontent. By the time he became the sole leader of the country in 1979, he had already sent thousands to prison, or early graves. And many more would meet that fate.

Saddam made a lot of crazy decisions after he assumed complete power, such as torturing and executing many of the top men in his own party, but probably the craziest thing he did was give his two emotionally unstable sons so much power.

Like Father, Like Sons

Uday was born in 1964 in Tikrit, while Saddam was in prison, and Qusay was born in 1966 months after his release. Although their mother Sajida spoiled both boys, there was no doubt that little Uday was her favorite.

The Iraqi dictator scoffed when his wife doted on the boys, especially Uday, who was his heir apparent. To compensate for the extra feminine attention, Saddam would bring his sons to military drills and—if they were really good—he'd even let them witness some torture sessions and executions!

Due to a combination of his poor parenting and inability to see the sociopaths that Uday and Qusay were, or possibly because of it, Hussein made the crazy decision of giving the two plenty of power and money.

Qusay was generally more laid back and less psychopathic than his older brother, although he was no angel. Qusay was given several responsibilities and positions by his father in the military and intelligence services, which he used to do his father's bidding.

One of the crazier things that Qusay did was to empty the marshes of southern Iraq to suppress the Shiite rebellion there in 1991. Although he did stop the rebellion temporarily, he also permanently destroyed the ecosystem and economy in that part of Iraq.

As crazy as Qusay was, though, Uday by far took the cake of crazy. At 6'6, Uday could be quite intimidating and he had no qualms about using his size to intimidate others to get what he wanted.

Uday liked to drive luxury sports cars, wear fine clothing and jewelry, and pick up attractive young women, whether they wanted to go with him or not.

Uday was described as fairly intelligent, if not unhinged. He invested in several businesses in Iraq, with government money, and was the owner of a professional soccer team in the 1980s. If you were a player on the team and didn't perform, you could expect to be locked in a cell, beaten, or both.

Perhaps one of the craziest things Uday Hussein did was murdering his father's "food taster," Kamel Gegeo, in front of several witnesses at a 1988 party. It turned out that Gegeo was responsible for introducing Saddam to his second wife, for whom he later left his first wife.

Ever the momma's boy, Uday had to avenge his mother's honor and because he couldn't kill his stepmother, he did the next best thing by killing Gegeo.

The combined acts of the Hussein boys was enough to drive a large segment of the Iraqi population against their father. Uday survived an assassination attempt in 1996, but neither of the Hussein brothers would survive when the Americans came to their house in 2003.

Although most Iraqis weren't necessarily happy with the American occupation of their country, few were sad to see the crazy Hussein brothers gone.

DID YOU KNOW?

- Qusay's son, Mustapha, was killed with the two brothers when soldiers from the 101st Airborne Division raided their Mosul home on July 22, 2003.

- Qusay was married with three children at the time of his death, while the playboy Uday reportedly married three times.

- After killing Gegeo, Uday fled to Switzerland and was sentenced to death, but he was later forgiven by his father.

- After falling out of favor with his father, Uday was relegated to the number two position. The more serious Qusay was also more popular with members of the Iraqi military and so was declared Saddam's successor in 2000.

- The US military found a treasure trove of interesting artifacts in Uday's Baghdad mansion, including pornography, HIV testing kits, dozens of luxury cars, several exotic animals, and a large gym with pictures of George Bush's daughters tapped to the wall.

FRANCOIS "PAPA DOC" DUVALIER:
THE VOODOO DICTATOR

All of the dictators we've profiled so far did some pretty crazy things that led to massive death tolls, the collapse of their regimes, or both. We've also seen that food and poverty were also often used as a weapon by dictators to either keep their populations in line or to punish a group within their countries.

Dictators also like to focus their crazy ideas on "others."

For Pol Pot, it was urban intellectuals and for Stalin, it was rural farmers. Hitler focused on the Jews and Slavs, while Idi

Amin reserved his vitriol for foreigners and other tribes within his country.

Francois "Papa Doc" Duvalier also demonized and persecuted "others" while he was the dictator of Haiti from 1957 to 1971, targeting the country's mulatto minority, communists, and non-Haitians in general.

He appealed to his people's patriotism and nationalism to gain plenty of support in the early years in his reign, which was bolstered by at least one attempted coup by some of the country's mulatto elite and American mercenaries.

But as with any other dictator, patriotism and nationalism are not enough; a healthy dose of fear is also needed.

Duvalier developed an intricate police state in Haiti that was based on the expansive police force he created and his image as a Voodoo priest. He knew that many of the Haitian people believed in Voodoo and if he could appeal to the darker elements of the religion, he could inspire fear in the people's hearts.

During his rule over Haiti, Duvalier is believed to have killed more than 6,000 people, with many of them taking place after elaborate Voodoo rituals.

When it was finally over, Duvalier's proved to be one of the most bizarre and brutal dictatorships in the Americas with his crazy policies and beliefs serving only to isolate and impoverish the already troubled Haiti even more.

Doctor Duvalier

Many think that Robert Duvalier's nickname, "Papa Doc," was related to his connection to Voodoo. Since Duvalier publicly identified himself with the top hat-wearing Voodoo spirit, Baron Samedi, many thought that was the connection to the nickname.

But Robert Duvalier really was a doctor.

Duvalier grew up in Haiti's capital of Port-au-Prince and although he didn't come from a privileged family, he was bright and ambitious enough to land a spot in medical school, graduating in 1934.

It may seem difficult to believe that as brutal and bizarre as Duvalier was, he was by all accounts a competent and thoughtful physician.

He was particularly concerned with stopping the spread of tropical diseases that were endemic in the Caribbean and took extra time to check on his patients, which earned him the nickname "Papa Doc."

As helpful as Papa Doc was in the hospitals and clinics of Port-au-Prince, his true calling was to rule in government and to use his Voodoo powers to eliminate his enemies.

After working for the government and then falling out of favor with the regime, Duvalier saw a chance to become president in 1957 on a pro-black, anti-communist platform. He won the election by taking more than 70% of the vote.

There were accusations of voter fraud, intimidation, and ballot stuffing from Duvalier's opponent, while others accused Papa Doc of using the dark arts to conjure demons that allowed him to win.

The reality is that he properly gauged the Haitian population's attitudes and was able to use a bit of demagoguery to get the black Haitians to "vote against" the mulattos.

Once Papa Doc took power, things immediately got crazy in Haiti.

Baron Samedi in Power

A failed 1958 coup by exiled Haitian military officers left Papa Doc extremely paranoid, leading him to unleash a whole torrent of crazy upon Haiti. Just as every dictator in modern history has done, Duvalier created a secret police force to root out his enemies. Papa Doc's force was known as the Tonton Macoute.

The Tonton Macoute were just as brutal as the KGB or Gestapo and certainly more bizarre.

The Tonton Macoute did the run-of-the-mill repression against Duvalier's enemies by abducting, torturing, murdering, and raping them, but they also took things to an entirely new level.

The victims' corpses were often left in public view for all to see and if family members attempted to bury their loved ones, they too became victims. But the strangest thing about the Tonton Macoute was its connection to Voodoo.

If you lived in Haiti during the 1960s and you saw a group of men wearing straw hats and denim shirts, and carrying machetes, come to your village, it was a good idea to hide because you were being visited by the Tonton Macoute.

Their unique style of dress was based on the Voodoo spirit Azaka Medeh, the protector of farmers; but their utilization of Voodoo went far beyond imagery.

Many of the captains of the Tonton Macoute were Voodoo priests and one in particular, Luckner Cambronne, earned the nickname the "Vampire of the Caribbean" because he was said to have drawn blood from his victims to sell and use in Voodoo rituals.

But it wasn't just Duvalier's secret police who engaged in the dark arts. Papa Doc also performed Voodoo rituals against his enemies.

Papa Doc had many of his enemies submerged live in sulfuric acid as he watched through peepholes from another room. And if there were any doubts as to whether or not Duvalier believed in the dark arts, an incident from early in his reign proves he did.

After having a heart attack in 1959, the already-paranoid Duvalier grew even more so and began to accuse those closest to him of planning a coup. Duvalier eventually had Clement Barbot, the head of the Tonton Macoute, charged with plotting to overthrow the government and had him imprisoned.

Papa Doc later had a change of heart and had Barbot released in 1963, but by that time, the former death squad leader *was* planning to overthrow his leader.

After Barbot failed in an attempt to kidnap Duvalier's children that year, Papa Doc ordered Barbot to be arrested and brought to him. But finding Barbot proved to be difficult, even on the small island, so Papa Doc thought greater things must be at work.

A Voodoo priest told Duvalier that Barbot was moving through the island disguised as a black dog, so Papa Doc ordered all the black dogs in Haiti to be killed! Barbot was later captured and killed, but he was very much in human form!

Duvalier's crazy repression and even crazier beliefs had the long-term effect of isolating Haiti from just about every country in the world. Although Duvalier was anti-communist and seemingly would have provided the United States with a base against Cuba for intelligence and a potential invasion, the Americans wanted nothing to do with the crazed Haitian dictator. Fidel Castro also rebuffed Duvalier's overtures.

By the end of Papa Doc's rule, Ethiopia was the only foreign country where he made an official state visit. No one else wanted to be the victim of a Voodoo curse.

DID YOU KNOW?

- In his quest to position black Haitians against the "others," Duvalier expelled the foreign-born bishops from Haiti, which earned him excommunication from the Roman Catholic Church.

- There is a story that Papa Doc cursed American President John F. Kennedy for withdrawing his support of Haiti. Duvalier later claimed that he made a Voodoo doll of Kennedy and stuck it 2,222 times with a needle. Papa Doc said that 22 was his lucky number.

- Many historians believe that Duvalier's hatred of mulatto Haitians came after the U.S. invasion and occupation of Haiti from 1915 to 1934. The Americans favored the mulatto minority and put them in power before leaving in 1934.

- Despite his generally negative feelings toward mulatto Haitians publicly and politically, his wife Simone came from a well-established mulatto family. They married in 1939, had four children, and remained married until Papa Doc's death in 1971.

- After dying of heart disease at the age of 64, Papa Doc was succeeded by his son, Jean-Claude "Baby Doc" Duvalier. Baby Doc was as crazy and brutal as his father, although he apparently the Voodoo spirits didn't work for him quite as well, as he was deposed and sent into exile in 1986.

KIM JONG-UN:

FOUR PACKS A DAY

Our next dictator, Kim Jong-Un of North Korea, is unique because he's still in power, so currently there's no telling how some of the crazy things he has done will impact his rule or his country. He inherited rule from his father, Kim Jong-Il, and appears to be just as dictatorial as him, but he also seems to want recognition from the West.

He invited former NBA star Dennis Rodman to be his personal guest and "peace envoy" and has engaged American

President Donald Trump in peace talks. And it actually seems that Jong-Un has reacted well to those overtures by all but is not stopping his militaristic bluster and missile tests.

But make no mistake about it, Kim Jong-Un has done plenty of crazy things since he took power in 2011. He has ordered the execution of several top North Korean officials, often by bizarre methods, was possibly behind the assassination of one of his brothers, and has generally continued to follow the pattern of repression and cult of personality instituted by his father.

Maybe more than anything, though, Kim Jong-Un follows a crazy health plan.

Many of the dictators we've profiled were actually health and fitness nuts, but Kim seems to have gone the other way. With all the power he has, he could afford to employ some of the best nutritionists and fitness trainers to keep him lean and mean, but the 5'6 Kim Jong-Un weighs in at a portly 300 pounds. The obese autocrat really doesn't seem to mind, though, as he imports expensive, fatty foods, such as cheese from Switzerland, and is said to smoke up to four packs of cigarettes a day.

With a family history of heart problems, some of the crazy things this dictator is doing seem to be to his own body.

Inheriting the Hermit Kingdom

Kim Jong-Un was born into a privileged life in the early 1980s in a country where poverty and repression are more common than anything, but since Kim's father was the leader, he was given access to things that most could only dream of.

Like leaving the country.

In the late 1990s and early 2000s, Kim lived in Switzerland under a pseudonym, which is where he acquired his love for Swiss cheese and basketball. He then came back to North Korea to study at university and work in the North Korean Communist Party, but it was known to everyone that he was merely being groomed to take his father's place.

Unlike most of our other dictators in this book, Kim never had to prove himself, never landed in prison due to his political activities, and never really had to risk anything to reach his current position.

North Korea, also known as the "hermit kingdom" because of its relative international isolation, was simply passed on to Kim Jong-Un after his father died. Sure he was prepared by his father and his father's most trusted men in many ways, but he was also woefully unprepared.

When Kim Jong-Un became North Korea's dictator, he inherited his father's crazy, violent ideas to go with his own crazy, unhealthy habits.

The Obese Autocrat

Kim Jong-Un made an immediate splash on the international scene by continuing his father's legacy of brutality. Kim became known for regularly purging high-ranking government and Communist Party officials and executing them in manners that are interesting, to say the least.

Once the reins of power were officially given to Kim, he did as any good dictator would do; by eliminating all competition. Kim executed 14 high-ranking officials in the government, including Vice Minister of the Army, Kim Chol, who was said to have been executed by mortar bombardment!

Kim later had his Uncle Jan Song-Thaek executed by firing squad and, in one of the more spectacular executions reported, had government official O Sang-Hon killed by a flamethrower!

But as crazy as the purges and executions Kim Jong-Un has ordered are, the way he treats his body is just as crazy.

In addition to his obesity, heavy smoking, poor diet, and family health problems, Kim Jong-Un is said to suffer from asthma, walks with a cane, and was reportedly on his deathbed in April 2020. None of this is good for a person of any age, but when one considers that Kim is only in his mid to late thirties, it will be a huge surprise if he makes it to 50.

And he doesn't appear to want to slow down.

Kim has been reported to spend more than $30 million a year on booze, and although he enjoys throwing lavish parties and doesn't drink all of that himself, he is known to consume several drinks of hard liquor per day.

If Kim doesn't watch himself, his crazy health habits will put him in an early grave and the mantle of power will pass to his sister, Kim Yo-Jong, making her the first female communist dictator in history.

DID YOU KNOW?

- Kim Yo-Jong was born in 1987, so she is about two to five years younger than Kim Jong-Un. The two are reported to be very close, but Yo-Jong has become a bit of an internet sensation with several memes floating around about her, so Jong-Un may have to worry.

- Kim Jong-Un married an attractive former cheerleader named Ri Sol-Ju in 2009. The couple has at least one child, although some news outlets claim they have up to three children.

- In addition to asthma and a family history of heart disease, Kim Jong-Un also has diabetes and high blood pressure.

- Kim Jong-Un increased North Korea's nuclear weapons program before meeting with Trump in 2018 and 2019, although they didn't reach any type of agreement.

- Kim Jong-Un allowed some North Korean athletes to compete with the South Korean team in the 2018 Winter Olympics in South Korea and allowed a limited concert of more than 150 South Korean K-Pop stars in North Korea in March of that same year.

MAXIMILIEN DE ROBESPIERRE:

FUN WITH THE GUILLOTINE

Revolutions are an interesting thing. They wipe away the old regime in way that often takes on a life of its own and, in the end, usually reflects the path that the revolution took before establishing a new regime. The Bolshevik Revolution in Russia in 1918 was born out of despair, poverty and violence and brought to that country an equally despairing and violent regime.

Although violent, the American Revolution was much less

brutal and, as a result, the government and society that rose from it have been remarkably stable.

Then there is the French Revolution.

The French Revolution began in 1789 with bright-eyed Enlightenment idealists who took a cue from America and saw their chance to right the wrongs that were occurring in their country.

They wanted to give more voting, property, and other rights to a greater segment of the population and they wanted to help alleviate the poverty and social divisions that were endemic at the time. But as the revolution dragged on, optimism was replaced with brutality.

The "Reign of Terror" was instituted by the revolutionaries in 1793 as a quick and violent means to forever wipe away the old traditions of the French monarchy and the Catholic Church. More than 16,000 Frenchmen and women were executed by the guillotine and another 40,000 were killed in the streets or languishing in prisons.

And behind it all was a man named Maximilien de Robespierre. Robespierre was the head of the Committee of Public Safety (basically the political police) during the Reign of Terror and ruthlessly ruled France from July 27, 1793 to July 28, 1794.

Not a very long reign, was it? Well, the reason for Robespierre's short time at the top was due to the very crazy decisions he made during the Reign of Terror. After being given a wide latitude by the French people to reform their country, he instead focused on settling old scores, enriching himself, and generally giving in to his sadistic impulses.

The crazy and violent decisions that Robespierre made eventually led to his demise in the same manner as many of the fellow countrymen he had condemned—underneath the guillotine.

Growing up in the Enlightenment

Maximilien François Marie Isidore de Robespierre, often just referred to as "Robespierre," was born in 1758 in France, which was a period of great change and social upheaval.

The religious wars of the 1600s were over and in their place; Western Europeans were making scientific advances and questioning the order of things in what is known as the Enlightenment. And France was ground zero for most of the Enlightenment.

Robespierre grew up under a monarchy and in a country with great disparities of wealth and social class on the one hand, but on the other hand, the writing of the philosophers Voltaire and Rosseau were widely read and available.

As a major follower of the general principles of the Enlightenment, Robespierre earned a law degree because he believed that would be the best way to affect change in France.

The young lawyer became a local activist and politician, advocating for social changes and changes to the constitution. Eventually, he caught the eye of more important activists and was asked to join the Jacobians, a society of radical Enlightenment thinkers.

By the time the French Revolution happened, Robespierre was leading the Jacobins and was a major player in the events that took place, but the problem with the French Revolution was that there were too many leaders. Once Louis XVI was overthrown and executed, most couldn't agree on what to do next.

Robespierre and his allies believed that only more violence was the answer, so when he became a member of the Committee of Public Safety in July 1793, he was finally able to mold France into his own perceived model.

Off with Everyone's Heads

The Reign of Terror was truly brutal, no doubt, but perhaps what made it even worse was its hypocrisy, which later played a major role in Robespierre's demise.

In October 1793, Robespierre really got the ball—and heads— rolling, when he began declaring enemy "conspirators" as those who opposed the ideals of the Revolution. Men and women were arrested and tortured, mostly without trial. If they did get a trial, it was usually little more than a formality before they were executed by the guillotine.

When others in the Committee thought the Reign of Terror should end, Robespierre responded by killing more people and going after what was left of the royals, such as Marie Antoinette, and imprisoning members of the Church and other notable people who weren't even against the initial Revolution.

It was too much for most of the French, but those closest to Robespierre were afraid to speak out lest they too were labeled "conspirators" and sent to the guillotine.

One thing that separates Robespierre from other brutal dictators is that he never denied his brutal acts and he in fact called for more.

After assuming total control of France, Robespierre let the world know just how crazy he was holding a "Festival of the Supreme Being." As the people of France cowered in fear and wondered where their next meals would come from, Robespierre put on an elaborate spectacle at great expense.

The purpose of the event wasn't exactly clear to most people. Robespierre said it was to celebrate a new religion that would replace the Catholic Church, but for most people, it had gone too far. It also seemed a lot like Robespierre was positioning himself to be god's replacement.

Robespierre's craziness was finally met with enough resistance when the Convention, which was the legislative assembly at the time, voted to arrest the despot and five of his closest followers.

Justice was much quicker for Robespierre than it was for many of his victims. He was arrested and executed by the guillotine the next day. For many in France, it was an ironic and poetic justice.

DID YOU KNOW?

- Robespierre was one of the shortest leaders in world history, standing at only 5'3. He sometimes wore shoes with heels to appear taller.

- Another crazy thing that Robespierre did was adopting the new "French Republican" calendar. Year one was 1792 and the months were renamed. Robespierre was executed in the month of "Thermidor."

- Robespierre never married and had no children. You could say that Maximilien was married to the Revolution.

- Among the many executions that Robespierre ordered was Georges Jacques Danton (1759–1794). Danton was actually once a good friend of Robespierre and a moderate revolutionary who wanted the Reign of Terror to end. He was accused of being too lenient toward the enemies of the revolution.

- The period immediately following Robespierre's execution until November 1, 1795, became known as the "Thermidorian Reaction." It marked a radical, often violent return to pre-Revolution ideas and the installation of a new government known as the "French Directory."

JUAN PERÓN:

JUST CHILLING
WITH THE NAZIS

Often thought of as just another Latin American *caudillio*, Argentine dictator Juan Perón is often overlooked in more popular histories in favor of other dictators. Sure, you probably vaguely remember that Madonna starred in a very forgettable musical about Perón and his wife titled *Evita*, but what do you really know about Juan Perón?

In most ways, he was pretty normal and far less brutal than

the other dictators in this book. Yes, Perón was a true dictator who employed repression and occasional violence to keep his hold on power, but he used those means far less than our other dictators.

Yet during his rule over Argentina from 1944 to 1955 and again from 1973 until his death in 1974, Perón managed to make some pretty crazy decisions that led to the downfall of his rule, split his political movement into factions, and ultimately ended with a brutal military regime in the 1970s and civil war.

Perhaps the craziest thing Juan Perón did; was to manage, or at least attempt to manage, a bizarre tight rope between Jews and former fascists. In a policy that historians today still don't completely understand, Perón accepted more Jewish refugees into Argentina after World War II than any other country in Latin America.

But he also gave thousands of Nazis and other fascist's asylum in Argentina. And make no mistake, many of these guys were some big names in fascist circles: Erich Priebke, Josef Mengele, and Ante Pavelic all made Argentina their home after World War II.

Sometimes those two communities butted heads, such as when former Nazi leader Adolf Eichmann was kidnapped by Israeli Mossad agents from a neighborhood in Buenos Aires in 1960. The intelligence that led to Eichmann's capture was provided by Argentine-Jews. Other less publicized incidents also happened.

In the end, the crazy and seemingly dissociative policy of allowing Jews and fascists to find asylum in Argentina became another piece in the puzzle of Perón's downfall. Neither group could help him when the inevitable came and both pointed toward his supposed implicit support of the other group as a legitimate reason for his removal from power.

Lucky in the Military, Unlucky in Love

Growing up in the town of Lobos, Argentina, Juan Domingo Perón always had a presence. He was tall, athletic, handsome, and charismatic. Young Juan never had problems meeting women or getting men to follow him, but unless you were a well-connected person at the top rungs of society, making your way in 1920s Argentina could be tough. So Juan, like many other young Argentine men in his position, joined the military and worked his way up the ranks rather quickly.

The problem with being in the Argentine military, though, was coups and military juntas were a regular part of life and if you didn't play with the right team, you were likely to be exiled, or worse.

So Perón lingered in military obscurity for a while because he didn't support the right team, which gave him time to focus on his personal life.

Perón met Aurelia Tizon in the 1920s and the two married in 1929, but she died of cancer in 1938. The marriage with Tizon was the beginning of a streak of bad luck that Perón had with women and marriages. His second marriage, while he was dictator, was to the well-known actress Eva "Evita" Duarte, but she also died of cancer.

In addition to two of his three wives dying of cancer, Perón had no children. The official Argentine line is that Perón was sterile, which in Latin America is an extremely emasculating label to have if you are a man, especially a man who is the leader of a country. It may have played a role in some of his later repressive activities, although there have been claims that he fathered illegitimate children.

As Perón struggled with his personal life in the 1930s, his professional life took a positive turn. He was back in with the good graces of the military and was sent to Europe to study military tactics in Italy, which allowed him to see the fascist regimes of Germany and Italy first-hand. Perón was truly impressed by what he saw, but he was quick to point out that Argentina was unique and couldn't necessarily institute the same system as those countries.

Perón's big break came when the military overthrew the president in 1943, instituting yet another military junta. But Perón had bigger plans—he wanted to be President.

Things started out well for Perón in 1946. He was a populist who knew how to whip crowds into a frenzy, yet he stayed away from demagoguery for most of his first term. With the help of Evita, he portrayed himself as a patriot who wished to keep Argentina out of the Cold War struggles and instead focus on internal reforms.

It worked, earning him a landslide victory.

But as Perón neared the end of his first term in 1952, he inched closer and closer to becoming a dictator. Perón had particular contempt for universities, so he had many closed down and had thousands of professors fired from their positions. He then focused on leaders of both left-wing and right-wing opposition parties, imprisoning, killing, and torturing anyone he perceived to be a threat.

By the time the 1952 election came, Perón easily won through a combination of intimidation, fraud, and repression.

Then there was that thing with the Nazis.

An Open Door Policy

Many believe that one of the craziest things Perón did while in power was giving asylum to so many fascists accused of war crimes, while simultaneously giving refuge to Jews fleeing Europe. The policy left Argentines divided, was one of the factors leading to his first downfall in 1955 and has made Argentina synonymous with Nazis to many people.

So why did Perón pursue this apparently crazy policy?

The answer to this question is as complex as Perón was himself. The Argentine dictator was never much of an anti-Semite. In fact, some of Perón's top government ministers and advisors, such as Raul Apold and Jose Bar Gelbard, were Jewish. Perón also didn't hesitate to recognize the State of Israel.

But Perón was also very open in his admiration for certain elements of fascism, especially the order the philosophy espoused, and he was an ardent anti-communist. Perón's political philosophy and movement, known as "Perónism," claims to follow a third political way that is neither communist nor capitalist, so to him, anyone who opposed the USA or USSR was a potential ally, Nazis included.

There were probably also practical reasons to give asylum to wanted fascists.

Many of these fugitive fascists had skills that Perón found useful for his own military and others had funds that they invested in Argentina. It should also be pointed out that there are large German-Argentine and Italian-Argentine communities who supported Perón during his rule, with some of them looking the other way when fascists landed in Argentina after World War II.

When Perón was removed from power in 1955, it was in the same way he assumed power, through a military coup. The country had become so divided through his economic policies that the event seemed inevitable to most.

Although the open door policy of giving asylum to Jews *and* fascists wasn't the deciding factor in the coup, it perhaps was symbolic of what was taking place.

Perón came out of exile in 1973 and briefly ruled before dying at the age of 78. His third wife briefly ruled before the government was turned over once more to a military junta and the country descended into what was known as the "Dirty War."

Today, Juan Perón is loved in many quarters of Argentine society and reviled in others, but to the rest of the world, he is remembered as the guy who made the decision to give the Nazis leaders asylum.

DID YOU KNOW?

- Evita Duarte-Perón was a well-known and beloved Argentine actress before meeting Juan. She was 24 years Juan's junior. Evita had naturally black hair, but she always dyed it blonde.

- Perón spent most of his exile from 1955 to 1973 in Francisco Franco's Spain (we'll get to Franco a bit). While in Spain, Perón demonstrated his political complexity once more by making connections with far-left and far-right political groups in Argentina before he returned.

- Among some of the more popular measures Perón enacted while president were a national minimum wage, an eight-hour workday, allowing women to vote, and socialized medicine.

- As part of his "third position" philosophy, Perón refused to join the International Monetary Fund (IMF). Argentina finally joined in 1956 after he was removed from power.

- Other repression methods that Perón employed were removing the justices of the Supreme Court and replacing them with those he chose.

BENITO MUSSOLINI:

MAYBE ROME WASN'T
ALL THAT GREAT

As we continue our voyage through the annals of the worst—
or best (depending on how you look at it)—dictators in
history, you'll notice that some made more crazy decisions
than others and some just made a few crazy decisions that
had major repercussions on history.

Our next dictator is one of the most recognizable despots in
world history. With his portly figure, uniform full of medals,

and trademark bald head, most people recognize Italian dictator Benito Mussolini as soon as they see him.

From the time that he and his paramilitary army took control of Rome in 1922; until he was brutally executed in 1943, Mussolini ruled Italy with an iron fist.

The Italian strongman was responsible for introducing the political philosophy of modern fascism to Europe and making it "mainstream" and for making an alliance with Nazi Germany that became known as the Axis Powers.

Many people would say that was by far the craziest thing.

There's no doubt that aligning with Nazi Germany was a crazy thing to do, but that in itself probably wouldn't have led to Mussolini's downfall and the destruction of large parts of Italy in the process. No, the craziest thing Mussolini did was thinking he could build a modern version of the Roman Empire.

One of the key tenets of fascism is the idealization of an earlier, "greater" time in a country's history. For Mussolini, the ideal time in Italy's history was the Roman Empire. It was during the Roman Empire when Italians ruled over millions of people in Europe, North Africa, and the Middle East. Mussolini thought that the Italian people would be behind his plan and, with German support, there was no stopping it.

But the dictator couldn't have been more wrong.

After Mussolini's military campaigns in North Africa and the Balkans failed; resulting in the Germans having to bail him out, he quickly lost influence with Hitler and the other Axis leaders. His own generals began to talk about him behind his back and worse, once he took Hitler's side, there was no going back.

Mussolini's crazy decision to build a Neo-Roman Empire not only lost him prestige, it also caused the Germans to relocate troops to North Africa, the Balkans, and eventually Italy, which in the end cost them the war. The crazy decision was certainly good for the allies, but it cost Mussolini his life and left his country in ruins.

Il Duce

To understand Benito Mussolini's crazy and destructive decision to try to rebuild the Roman Empire, it's important to understand his outlook on life. Perhaps no world leader embodied fascism more than Mussolini; this includes Hitler since Mussolini was in power before the German dictator.

But he wasn't a diehard fascist from the start.

Mussolini actually began his political life on the left wing and was active in several socialist groups before World War I. The war, though, split socialists around the world. Although many socialists were generally anti-war, some believed that defeating Germany, monarchism, and imperialism was more important. Mussolini was not one of those socialists.

He was quite vocal about his support for Italy to join World War I on the Allies' side against Germany and Austria-

Hungary, particularly against the latter, where he hoped the Italians would gain back lost land. To Mussolini's socialist friends, he was sounding more and more like a nationalist and an imperialist, so he was kicked out of the Italian Socialist Party.

It really didn't matter to Mussolini, though, because he had a war to fight.

Mussolini was severely wounded in battle, which left him with physical and mental scars but earned him the street cred of nationalists across Italy. When Mussolini formed the National Fascist Party, thousands flocked to join and hear the speeches of "Il Duce" (the leader), as he became known.

Things moved so quickly that on October 28, 1922, Mussolini was able to lead a force of 30,000 of the most faithful of his party, and the most violent, known as the "Black Shirts," on the "March on Rome." They demanded the government be turned over to them, and it was the next day!

Everything was going well for Il Duce, but like all dictators, he started to believe his own hype.

In the Shadow of Julius Caesar

Mussolini made no secret about his plan to create a new Roman Empire. He gave several speeches about it and made several not-so-veiled threats toward the British and French relating to their North African possessions. Il Duce thought that he'd be able to roll over the smaller countries in North

Africa and the Balkans, but he probably should have rethought the crazy idea after 1937.

In 1935, Mussolini invaded the northeast African nation of Abyssinia (Ethiopia) over what he said were border violations by that country with Italy's colonies in the region. Italy was able to beat Abyssinia, but it took two years, cost the lives of more than 10,000 Italian soldiers, and was a public relations disaster for Mussolini, Italy, and fascism in general.

Still, Mussolini went forward with his plans to build the new Roman Empire.

After World War II began, Italy joined Germany in the Axis Powers. As Il Duce watched the Germans take country after country, he decided it was a good time to move. He ordered Italian troops to invade British-held Egypt from Italian Libya in September 1940 and the next month he ordered an invasion of the Balkans from Italy.

Both campaigns were disasters for Italy, and although the Axis Powers were able to take the Balkans, it was only after the Germans, Croatians, and Bulgarians sent a sizable number of troops to the front and at a great human cost.

As for North Africa, command of the Italian forces was handed over to German Field Marshal Irwin Rommel, and although the Italian forces generally acquitted themselves well on the battlefield, they were for the most part underequipped and ill-prepared for a major campaign against the British.

It was a truly crazy decision by Mussolini to try to rebuild the Roman Empire overnight. The failed campaigns also basically sidelined Mussolini politically for the remainder of the war, which was quite a blow to the dictator's ego. Worse yet for him, but good for the Allies, it marked the beginning of the end of the Axis advance in Europe.

It was a defensive war after that and Italy would be the site of major fighting in 1943 during the Anzio campaign.

When Mussolini was about to be executed on April 28, 1945, by a leftwing partisan firing squad, he probably thought to himself, "Man, that Roman Empire thing was some crazy sh*t!"

DID YOU KNOW

- When the Allies invaded Italy in 1943, support for Mussolini quickly dried up, especially in the south. The Nazis attempted to keep Mussolini in power by setting up a government called the Italian Social Republic based in the city of Salo, but a partisan rebellion brought it down on April 25, 1945.

- Mussolini's first wife, Ida, died in 1937 from a brain hemorrhage, although many believe it was caused by Fascist Party officials. All records of the marriage were destroyed and the son they had together was imprisoned in a mental hospital and later murdered.

- Mussolini stood about 5'6, which isn't too short, but his tendency to gain weight made him appear portlier.

- He had five children with his second wife, Rachele. One of Il Duce's granddaughters, Alessandra Mussolini, has worked as a top model and has held elected office in the Italian and European parliaments.

- The idea of building a new Roman Empire was so important to Mussolini that he gave the quest a name, *spazio vitale*, which means "living space" or "vital space."

HIDEKI TOJO:

WAKING THE SLEEPING GIANT

It should be clear to you by now that one of the craziest things you can do if you ever become a dictator is to start a war with countries before you're ready to do so, and under no means should you ever consider invading Russia. But Russia isn't the only country that it'd be crazy to invade.

The United States is nearly as large as Russia, has more people, and in 1941 was much wealthier, despite suffering from the Great Depression. Add to that the fact that the US was much more cohesive and homogenous in 1941, it has some pretty drastic topographical diversity, and nearly every American owns a gun, it would seem like suicide to start a war with that place.

But that was exactly the crazy decision Japanese Prime Minister/dictator Hideki Tojo made when the Japanese Navy attacked Pearl Harbor on December 7, 1941.

Many historians see it as one of the biggest military and political blunders of the 20th century, right up there with Nazi Germany's invasion of the Soviet Union.

When Japan attacked Pearl Harbor, American sentiment towards participating in World War II wasn't especially high. Most Americans thought those were European and Asian affairs and there was organized resistance to American involvement led by Charles Lindbergh and other notable Americans.

Before Pearl Harbor, America was a sleeping giant. It was numerically, economically, and industrially strong, but for the most part, far removed from the major conflicts of the world.

However, Tojo was a firm believer in Japan's militaristic ideology, the divinity of the emperor, and the supremacy of the Japanese people. He also harbored a special loathing for Americans, who he thought were lazy, weak, and would put up no real defense. So when Tojo was given complete command of Japan's military and civilian government in 1941, he went full steam ahead with the attack on US soil.

The result, of course, was the complete devastation of Japan, which ended with the dropping of the atomic bombs on Hiroshima and Nagasaki in 1945. And just like the other dictators we've profiled who made the crazy decisions to invade countries that would've been better left alone, the move brought about Tojo's downfall. He was executed by an Allied tribunal in 1948.

Tojo should've let the giant sleep!

All Work and No Play Makes You the Dictator of Japan

There was nothing necessarily remarkable about Hideki Tojo that would've made anyone who knew him as a child believe that he was going to have a dramatic impact on world history. His father's family was descended from the Samurai, which positioned him for a career in the military, while his mother came from a devout Buddhist family.

Young Hideki wasn't the brightest student, but he was usually the hardest worker, choosing to stay after class and spend most of his free time studying. He was actually pretty much a party pooper, which never gained him any friends though it did help his career in the military.

After seeing action in Russia in the early 1900s, Tojo was poised to become one of the leaders in the new Japan that was emerging in the 1930s. It was a Japan that was strongly anti-communist, allied with the fascist states of Germany and Italy, and was highly imperialistic.

The Japanese government planned to create an empire called the Greater East Asia Co-Prosperity Sphere, but for the most part, the only people who would prosper were the Japanese. One of the first countries incorporated into the Sphere was Manchuria, which was ruled by Japan from 1919 to 1945. One of Tojo's first major assignments in the military high command was to command the Kenpeitai (Japanese military police) in Manchuria.

It was Tojo's first taste of dictatorial power, which he apparently relished. He rooted out all resistance to the Japanese occupation. The exact numbers of Manchurian civilians killed during the Japanese occupation is still being debated, but many say it was at least one million.

Tojo's activities in Manchuria and his workaholic behavior earned him the praise of his superiors, so by 1940 he was in command of the military and second to the Prime Minister. Although the Japanese government was technically still a democracy at the time, the Prime Minister essentially had dictatorial powers and was second only to Emperor Hirohito.

Still, there were two major factions within the government: those who wished to negotiate with the United States and those who wished to go to war. Tojo was the head of the war faction.

Americans Are All Weak and Lazy

Hideki Tojo's experience with Americans was somewhat limited, although he probably had more interactions with them than many of his countrymen did at the time.

After serving as a military attaché for the Japanese

government in Germany from 1919 to 1922, Tojo traveled home via steamer across the Atlantic, then a transcontinental train in the United States before taking another steamer across the Pacific.

Needless to say, he wasn't impressed with the American people.

Being the consummate workaholic that he was, he looked with disgust on the Americans who were drinking, partying, and generally having a good time. To Tojo, this proved that all Americans were decadent, weak, lazy, and generally soft.

It should be pointed out that Tojo's time in America was quite limited and he only stayed in the larger cities. It was also the "Roaring 20s," so his view of the American people was quite skewed. Most Americans were hardworking farmers, factory workers, and small businessmen who were nothing like the Americans he met in the cities and on the trains.

That mattered little to Tojo, though, and as his star began to shine brighter in the Japanese government, he became the leading voice of war. The American government enacted sanctions and embargos on Japan for its occupation of Manchuria and Indochina and its war with China, so Tojo argued that the only option was a quick first strike.

When Tojo was elevated to Prime Minister on October 17, 1941, he only had to convince the emperor that attacking Pearl Harbor was a good idea.

After the tide of the war went against Japan, Tojo was relieved of his office by the military in 1944, but the damage had been done. Japan fought on for another year and when the Americans finally came to Tokyo, Tojo attempted to kill himself with a gunshot to the heart but failed.

He was tried, convicted, and executed by hanging in 1948. Tojo's fate probably could have been avoided if he just hadn't made the crazy decision to attack Pearl Harbor.

DID YOU KNOW?

- Although Tojo would be considered shorter than average for men today at only 5'4, he was taller than the average Japanese soldier at the time; who only stood 5'3.

- Like most dictators, Tojo had a nickname. He became known as "Razor Tojo" due to his quick rise in the military and government; the name also has a tough and scary ring to it.

- Tojo married his wife Kotsuko in 1909. The couple had seven children—three sons and four daughters.

- While Tojo was being held in a prison before his trial, an American dentist inscribed the message "Remember Pearl Harbor" in Morse code on his teeth.

- Similar to Mussolini, Tojo's tomb has become a pilgrimage destination for ultra-nationalists.

FIDEL CASTRO:

EMPTYING THE PRISONS

Cuban dictator Fidel Castro was well-known throughout the world. He led his country for 52 years, making him the longest-serving head of state in modern times. Of course, he was also known for a numerous other interesting, important, and very crazy things.

Castro was friends and comrades with the famous Argentine revolutionary Che Guevara, as the two men led the revolution that brought Castro to power in 1959.

The Cuban dictator is also remembered for being the centerpiece of the 1962 Cuban Missile Crisis and for earning the ire of American President John F. Kennedy and the United States. That opposition to the US earned him at least a couple of assassination attempts and cut his country off from the superpower that is only about 90 miles away.

Castro's seemingly successful opposition to the US earned him the respect of leaders throughout the developing world, who loved seeing the "Yankees" get taken down a notch, but make no mistake about it, Castro was a brutal despot.

As with many of communist dictators, Castro's utopian ideals quickly descended into violence and brutality. He was known for mass executions by firing squads, which he called "el paredon" or "the wall," and for extreme censorship and repression that turned the beautiful Caribbean island into a prison.

Castro truly did some repressive and crazy things, but emptying Cuba's prisons may have been one of the craziest things he did.

From 1976 to 1980, Jimmy Carter was the President of the United States. The liberal Democrat Carter signaled to Cuba that he was open to normalizing relations between the two countries.

Travel restrictions were lifted and everything appeared to be going well, but then thousands of Cubans began rushing various embassies for asylum. Then on April 21, 1980, Castro said that any Cuban who wanted to leave the country could do so at their own cost through the port of Mariel.

The announcement caused a rush of emigration that became known as the "Mariel Boatlift."

Castro used the Mariel Boatlift to get rid of many of his political enemies and to empty the prisons, but in the end, it proved to hurt him more than it helped. Americans weren't too thrilled about having to care for nearly 125,000 refugees, up to 20,000 of which were criminals.

The Mariel Boatlift is seen as one of the many reasons why Jimmy Carter lost the 1980 presidential election to Ronald Reagan, which was bad news for Castro. Once the conservative, anti-communist Republican came into office, he ended the normalization process, went back to the old travel restrictions, and generally isolated Cuba once again.

Castro would have to wait until the end of the Cold War before his country opened to the rest of the world, and to top things off, many of the Cuban Boatlift criminals were deported from the US and ended up back in Cuba.

Baseball and Communism

Fidel Alejandro Castro Ruz was born in 1926 to a wealthy sugar plantation family in rural Cuba. Castro's not-so-humble origins may seem a bit ironic since he later became such an avowed Marxist, although often times the leaders of Marxist and communist movements were more or less privileged individuals who were able to attend good schools and universities.

And that was the case with Fidel.

Young Fidel was introduced to Marxist philosophy while studying at the University of Havana in the 1940s, and before too long, he was active in a variety of organizations that were all about sticking it to the "Yankees" and their colonial lackeys in the Caribbean and Latin America.

Besides Marxism-communism, Castro's other love was baseball!

He may have hated the Yankee imperialists, but he sure loved their national sport. As he became active in leftwing student groups at the University of Havana, Castro played baseball for the school's team and was said to be quite a pitcher. The future dictator even had dreams of playing in the big leagues, or at least professionally in the Cuban league.

But when Castro went up against top competition, he soon learned that he wouldn't make his mark on the world in baseball, so he went to law school where he made even more connections in leftist circles.

Castro eventually decided that violent revolution was the only way to remove rightwing dictator Fulgencio Batista from power.

The 1950s could've ended up any number of ways for Castro—he could've been killed during the revolution or drifted into obscurity—but thanks to some luck and the foresight to choose the guerilla tactician Guevara as his right-hand man, he came out on top in 1959.

After that, Castro ruled Cuba through several different positions—Prime Minister, President, and head of the Communist Party—until he retired in 2011.

And during those decades in power, he did plenty of brutal and crazy things.

The Mariel Boatlift

Like Mugabe, when Castro first came to power, most people around the world wanted to see him succeed. Batista was known to be corrupt and brutal and Cuba was viewed as a place with great potential.

It didn't take long for Castro to change all that.

The firing squads began almost immediately and continued around the clock until 1961. Although Castro tried to hide the knowledge of the firing squads, the world eventually found out.

The nearly constant firing squads were written about in the press and were even featured in a 1961 *Twilight Zone* episode titled "The Mirror," where Robert Falk plays a paranoid dictator who resembled Castro down to the goatee and military fatigues.

To stay true to his Marxist-communist beliefs, Castro severely restricted the Catholic Church in Cuba and imprisoned any known Jehovah's Witnesses. He also limited movement within the country, controlled the press and imprisoned or assassinated any political opposition.

Now all of that is truly bad and makes Castro one of the worst dictators on any list. He is estimated to be responsible for up to 100,000 deaths, which in a country of only about 11 million people, is quite a high number.

But the Mariel Boatlift was perhaps the craziest decision Castro made because it set American public opinion, and ultimately the US government, against him. The American people were gripped with fear that a wave of Cuban criminals would flow across the US, although it's estimated that only about 2,700 hardened criminals entered the country as part of the Boatlift. The rest of the 20,000 "criminals" were usually in prison for minor offenses or they were political opponents of the Castro regime.

In the end, the Mariel Boatlift became a political football that Castro, Carter, and Reagan all tried to pass and punt among themselves.

Castro thought that, by letting the prisoners go, he'd alleviate many of his problems and keep improving relations with the Americans, but in the end, it proved to be just another crazy decision that backfired.

DID YOU KNOW?

- Fidel's brother, Raul, took over control of Cuba after he resigned in 2011. Raul is still in office, while Fidel died in 2016 at the age of 90.

- The term "Marielito" is used to refer to those who came over on the Muriel Boatlift.

- President Reagan probably gained the most politically from the Muriel Boatlift. The images of the boatlift helped solidify his rightwing support in many parts of the US, but by giving public messages of support for the Marielitos, he was able to consolidate his support with the more conservative Republican Miami-Cuban community.

- Refugee camps were established throughout southern Florida, which included the Orange Bowl.

- Tony Montana is perhaps the most famous Marielito. In case you somehow don't know who Tony Montana is, he is the fictional crime lord played by Al Pacino in the 1983 film *Scarface*.

FRANCISCO FRANCO:

KEEPING SPANISH WOMEN BAREFOOTED AND PREGNANT

All of the dictators profiled in this book, no matter their political stripes, used repression of one sort or another to hold power. It was often directed at their enemies, sometimes illogically, and often with disastrous results. Spanish dictator Francisco Franco was also no stranger to repression and the occasional crazy decision.

The lifelong military man came to power in 1939 after the

nationalists defeated the republicans in the Spanish Civil War. Franco instituted a rightwing dictatorship that had all the trappings of fascism, yet he was careful not to go too far down that road.

Franco instituted political repression that was considered to be extreme and crazy even by some Nazis who visited Spain in the 1930s, but he never signed onto the Axis alliance, which allowed his regime to survive World War II. In fact, Franco ruled Spain until he died in 1975, a relic of the past that most in Europe wanted to forget.

But Spaniards can't forget everything that happened during the Spanish Civil War and Franco's regime, and have to live with the legacy of the war and some of Franco's crazy decisions.

One of the crazy things Franco did that had long-lasting repercussions was his policy toward women. To say Franco was old fashioned with gender roles would be a bit of an understatement. The decrees he passed kept women out of most professions, outlawed their political activities and right to vote, and even limited their abilities to have bank accounts.

Franco believed that good Spanish women should be barefooted and pregnant.

But even many of the pregnant women during his regime still faced problems. Due to their political affiliations or any number of other reasons, many pregnant women had their newborns taken from them. Tens of thousands of Spanish children were born in orphanages during the 1940s and '50s, creating a generation of lost souls.

Some scholars believe that this act alone set Spain back decades behind the rest of Europe.

El Paquito

Francisco Franco Bahamonde was seemingly born with a silver spoon in his mouth in 1892, but his life took a more circuitous route than originally seemed likely. Franco came from a long line of proud Spanish naval officers.

He could point to ancestors who helped build the Spanish Empire in the Americas and others who fought in the Spanish Armada against the British in a valiant but losing effort.

Things were all set for Franco to follow in his father's and ancestors' footsteps by becoming a naval officer, but then the Spanish-American War happened.

As a result of the war, the Spanish lost most of their fleet.

Still wanting a career in the military, Franco entered the army at the age of 14.

Life in the army wasn't easy at first for Franco. He was teased by his fellow recruits for his young age, small frame, and 5'3 stature, earning the nickname "El Paquito" or "Little Franc." But the future leader proved to have a thick skin, which gained him points in the eyes of his superior officers. Franco also demonstrated a keen memory and an aptitude for military life.

By the 1920s, young Franco was well on his way to a rewarding career in the military.

After impressing the Spanish high command in action in Spanish North Africa, Franco was promoted to Colonel and eventually General. The political situation began to fall apart in Spain in the 1930s, though, as it did throughout most of the rest of the world. Spain was adversely affected by the Great Depression, which allowed a leftwing government to come to power in 1936.

The military, the Catholic Church, nationalists, and fascists weren't happy with the turn of events so they decided to go to war.

The ever pragmatic yet politically astute Franco took advantage of the situation by organizing the sometimes opposing groups on the rightwing into a powerful army and later the political movement known as 'The Falange'.

Franco's time in power began with some of the worst repressions and "paybacks" ever seen in an authoritarian regime. The leftwing government imposed its own brand of oppression known as the "Red Terror," which was primarily directed against the Church, often against Church leaders who were, for the most part, apolitical.

The Red Terror left thousands dead, was the primary catalyst for the Civil War, and led to the Franco nationalist government's own version of repression known as the "White Terror."

The White Terror was extremely more directed than the violence of the Red Terror. Leftist leaders were singled out for torture and murder, ultimately leaving between 50,000 and 200,000 people dead across Spain.

Among those singled out were Republican/leftist women. To Franco, they were the worst sort of revolutionaries because they not only didn't have the right ideas, but they also didn't know their place.

So Franco embarked on a years-long campaign to show women their proper roles in Spanish society.

Women Are Mothers, Not Workers

It's crazy to think of a modern society where women aren't allowed to vote, work, or even have bank accounts, but this was all true in Spain into the early 1970s, which really isn't that long ago. Even Nazi Germany and Fascist Italy accorded women more political and social rights than Franco did for Spain's women.

As soon as Franco took power, he initiated his anti-feminist crusade through a combination of state-sponsored propaganda, laws, and police-state repression.

The mode of propaganda was just like you'd find in any other authoritarian regime in the world at the time. Posters, films, and later television told the dangers of feminism and how feminism led to drug use, sedition, and other anti-social behaviors.

The Franco government's definition of feminism was basically any activity by women other than motherhood. A woman didn't have to be Susan B. Anthony or Gloria Steinem to fall into the feminist category in Francoist Spain.

The laws instituted were directed at keeping women out of the workplace. Other than servant/maid positions, it became almost impossible for women to find work outside of the home in the early years of Franco's rule and nearly impossible for former Republican women to do so.

The policies against women in the workplace led to some of Franco's first real problems. In the late 1950s and early 1960s, due to the population decline from the Civil War, there was a labor shortage in Spain. The dictatorship had a difficult time attracting foreigners to work there who were considered compatible with its social ideals, so the economy lagged for several years.

Finally, Franco relented and allowed more women to enter the job force in the early 1960s.

And when all else failed, Franco wasn't afraid to use good old police state tactics to keep women in line.

More than 30,000 Republican mothers had their children removed from them in the 1940s and '50s and more than 15,000 were imprisoned during the Civil War and in the first few years after it ended. Some of Spain's top female artists and writers were forced into exile during the period, with many never returning.

Franco's female policies were one of the many reasons that Spain remained isolated for his entire rule. Realizing that this was the case, Franco did relent on some of the more repressive laws regarding women in the early 1970s, but the damage had already been done.

DID YOU KNOW?

- In Franco's Spain abortion was illegal and women who had an abortion performed faced prison time. Abortion for extraordinary reasons wasn't legalized until 1985 in Spain. Abortion for birth control wasn't legalized in Spain until 2010.

- Adultery by women was a crime punishable by jail time in Francoist Spain.

- Divorce also wasn't an option until the end of Franco's rule.

- Franco married his wife Carmen in 1923. They had one child, a girl named Maria.

- Franco's Spain became a haven for former Nazis, authoritarians, and other wanted people. Notable Nazi Otto Skorzeny lived on and off in Spain until his death in 1975, and Argentine dictator Juan Peron lived in Franco's Spain during his exile.

- Franco died on November 20, 1975, at the age of 82.

MAO ZEDONG:

OLD PEOPLE SUCK

Modern China is often viewed as somewhat of a miracle society. It went from a hardcore, repressive dictatorship with a closed society and economy, to a wider, more open and economically successful economy in just a couple of decades. Of course, no one will say China isn't without many problems today.

It's still a one-party state, dissidents are routinely thrown in jail, and the government tightly controls the press and Internet.

On the other hand, though, things are very different than they were in the 1970s. Outsiders can visit China and millions of non-Chinese live and work in the communist country. Likewise, Chinese citizens are allowed to leave and freely travel, acquire wealth, and have a level of freedom they haven't enjoyed since the inception of the communist regime.

Communist China was ruled by Mao Zedong from the time it was born in the ashes of the Chinese Civil War in 1949 until his death in 1976. During that time, Mao made some pretty crazy decisions that cost millions of people their lives, the two worst being the "Great Leap Forward" and the "Cultural Revolution."

When it comes to trying to pick which of the two was crazier, it's hard to say.

The Great Leap Forward, which was Mao's plan to industrialize China into a Soviet-style communist state from 1958 to 1962 was an unmitigated disaster and a humanitarian nightmare of an epic scale. The program collectivized private land (remember Stalin?) and forced people to work in factories. The result was a famine that killed between 18 and 45 million people.

The Great Leap Forward was truly a crazy decision and one that Mao should have avoided given Stalin's human-made famine 20 years earlier. But they say the mark of insanity is when one keeps trying to do the same thing over and over expecting different results.

But as crazy as the Great Leap Forward was, the Cultural Revolution was probably a bit crazier. You see, the failure of the Great Leap Forward temporarily sidelined Mao, but once he came back into favor with the Communist Party, he did so with a vengeance.

Mao appealed to the young communists of China to destroy everything old. From Confucian and Buddhist temples to writings of the previous generation of communist intellectuals, anyone and everything that was considered old was subject to destruction.

By the time the Cultural Revolution was over when Mao died in 1976, up to 20 million Chinese had died, thousands of ancient temples and shrines had been destroyed, universities had been closed, and some of the brightest minds in China were either dead or exiled.

It took China more than a decade to recover from the Cultural Revolution, and in many ways, it's still recovering.

Chairman Mao

Unlike some of the communist dictators in our book, Mao Zedong really did come from a poor family. He grew up in the sticks of the Hunan province. After moving to Beijing to attend university, Mao learned first-hand that he came from a different class and background to many of his classmates.

Due to his background, Mao found it difficult to make friends with many of his more urban and upper-class classmates, but he found solace in the writings of Marx and the theories of communism and anarchism.

Mao played a leading role in the establishment of the Communist Party of China in the early 1920s but also made connections with the nationalist movement, though he eventually saw them as too "reactionary." The two groups initially sought to work together to establish a government after the collapse of the Qing Dynasty and the abdication of the last emperor, but it wasn't meant to be.

The communists and nationalists engaged in a civil war for control of China from 1927-1937 and then aligned against the Japanese through World War II before reigniting their war from 1946 to 1949.

It was during the Chinese Civil War that Mao became the leader of communist China by introducing successful guerilla tactics to his army, eventually driving the nationalists to live on the island of Formosa.

And that's what's important to know about Mao. Yes, he was a fairly intellectual guy, but he was also pragmatic and knew that true power only came with force or the threat of it.

Violence was a tool that Mao used to achieve power, and once he was in power, he had no qualms about using it to stay in power.

Leading the Youth

Mao's Great Leap Forward was such a crazy decision and a disaster that he actually stepped down as the Chairman of the People's Republic of China, although he maintained his position as the Chairman of the Communist Party of China. Since China was a one-party state, and he was the head of that one party, Mao still held most of the power in the country.

But it was *almost* an admission of failure and most certainly felt like a loss of face.

By late 1966, Mao declared that the old leaders of China had grown decadent and had lost their way and were no longer following true Marxism. He said that the only way to remedy this situation was by handing the reins of power over to the youth.

Although the speeches he gave were dressed in standard Marxist-communist platitudes, many believe that there were personal reasons for him leading the Cultural Revolution.

Mao blamed others more than himself for the failure of the Great Leap Forward, so when he initiated the Cultural Revolution in 1966, it was a way for him to get some payback and reestablish his position as the most important person in China.

The Cultural Revolution began with his paramilitary "Red Guards" beating, humiliating, and arresting a long list of Mao's enemies. This was followed by purges in the government and military that saw thousands imprisoned and killed.

Within a few weeks, the Cultural Revolution turned into a bizarre spectacle of mob violence that spared no one, especially those over the age of 30.

Students called their professors and teachers out as enemies of Mao and children informed on their parents. A general sense of fear and doom hung over all of China, from the largest cities where most of the action was taking place to the rice paddies of the south.

The slogan of the Cultural Revolution became the destruction of the "Four Olds," which were: old customs, old culture, old habits, and old ideas.

In other words, anything related to Chinese culture before 1949 was targeted for destruction. Although that often mean tombs, temples, and statues, it could also include anyone who was born before the Chinese Civil War.

At the height of the Cultural Revolution from 1968 to 1971, China was virtually isolated from the rest of the world. It had previously cut ties with the Soviet Union over differences in Marxist doctrine and it was an avowed enemy of the "imperialist" United States.

Needless to say, the Cultural Revolution didn't help China's standing in the world.

The immense death toll of the Cultural Revolution came through a combination of massacres, mass arrests, and cumulative executions, but damage to supply lines also caused starvation and even cannibalism in some places.

In addition to the millions of lives lost and the brain drain Mao's crazy decision to lead the Cultural Revolution cost China, modern scholars believe that the majority of China's pre-Communist Era artifacts were destroyed or looted and sold on the international market.

No price can be put on the loss of those cultural objects.

DID YOU KNOW?

- The Cultural Revolution really didn't hurt Chinese-US relations. As Mao urged young communists to fight for Marxist ideals on the streets of Beijing and the other major cities, he met with American President Richard Nixon in 1972. The two countries re-normalized their relations in 1979.

- Later leaders of China realized just how crazy the Cultural Revolution was. They have consistently tiptoed around condemning it outright because to do so would be to condemn Mao, but it is rarely mentioned in official texts.

- "Maoism" is the strain of Marxist-communist thought that gives primacy to the peasant instead of the worker/proletariat. During the middle of the Cultural Revolution, Mao sent many of the Red Guards and other young communists to the countryside to learn how it was to live and work as a true peasant, although skeptics say it was to move the violent and rebellious leaders of the movement to areas where they had less impact.

- Another consequence of the Cultural Revolution is that it created more social differences in China. Although theoretically a communist society is supposed to be free of class differences and the Cultural Revolution was intended to bring China into a period of true communism, it instead created a new, privileged class of young Chinese.

- Mao died of a heart attack on September 9, 1976, in Beijing at the age of 82. He was survived by his fourth wife and at least three children, although the status of some of his other ten children was not known.

AYATOLLAH KHOMEINI:
HE REALLY HATED THAT BOOK

It would be an understatement to say that the West and Islam have had a complicated relationship. After Muhammad, the founder of Islam, died in 632 CE, the religion underwent a rapid and often violent expansion into Christian territories. Muslim forces conquered parts of the Christian Byzantine Empire and even conquered Spain and threatened France before being driven south in 732 CE.

Christian Europe then went on the offensive in the 11th

century beginning with the Crusades and the "Reconquista" of Spain from the 8th to the 15th centuries, before the Islamic Ottoman Empire conquered the Byzantine Empire in 1453 and took large parts of southeastern Europe in the process.

The nations of the West were ascendant in much of the modern period, with Britain, France, and (to some extent) Spain colonizing much of the Islamic world.

After World War II, things were quiet until Israel became a nation in 1948, then the idea of the West versus the Islamic world was renewed with some new players on the chessboard.

When Islamic fundamentalists took over Iran in 1979, they immediately raised tensions between the West and Islam up 100 levels, adding new political and religious dimensions to the conflict.

Although Iranians are ethnically Persian and not Arabs, and Iran is Shiite Islamic country, with the Shiites being the minority sect in Islam, it is a fundamentalist country that strictly follows Islamic or Sharia Law. Many devout Muslims respected the Iranians' adherence to Islamic law as well as how they stuck it to the West when radical students took over the American embassy in Tehran.

Iran instituted a new constitution in 1979 and rebranded itself as the Islamic Republic of Iran. The head of this new theocracy was a man named Sayyid Ruhollah Khomeini, although, to most of the world, he was just known as the Ayatollah (leader) Khomeini.

Khomeini was certainly unique for a modern dictator when he took the reins of power in 1979. Unlike other modern Islamic dictators who wore Western attire and often made connections with either the Western or Communist blocs, Khomeini wore traditional Persian garb and was as anti-Soviet as he was anti-American.

The Americans may have been imperialist Christians, but the Soviets were equally bad as godless atheists.

During his 20 years in power, Khomeini said and did a lot of crazy things.

By angering both West and East with his rhetoric and calls for jihad, he isolated Iran, which played a major role in its loss of up to 700,000 people in the Iran-Iraq War. Although Iran was larger and had more people than Iraq, the Iraqis were better supplied through their connections with both the East and West.

During the Iran-Iraq War, Khomeini threw human waves of suicide squads at the Iraqis, many of them child soldiers. This only served to isolate Iran further.

And of course, Khomeini was just as repressive as any of the other dictators on this list, imprisoning, torturing, and killing his opponents. As bad as those things all are, they're to be expected with most dictators. No, the craziest thing Khomeini did was when, in 1988, he ordered a *fatwa* or death sentence on Salman Rushdie for writing the book *The Satanic Verses*.

The death sentence was never carried out, but it had the effect of further isolating Iran from the rest of the world until

Khomeini died in 1989. Khomeini's fatwa also proved to be very polarizing, pitting the Islamic world against the West like never before. In fact, many point toward the controversy as the origin of the current West-Islamic conflict.

From One Dictator to Another

Iran, also known as Persia, has a long and illustrious history. When Alexander the Great conquered the Achaemenid Persian Empire in 331 BCE, it had already been around for more than 200 years. Before that, the Elamites called Persia their home and after the Achaemenids, the Parthian and Sassanian dynasties ruled Iran/Persia.

After the Arab Muslims conquered the Sassanids in the 7th century CE, Persia became a Shiite Islamic land, but its culture was still great. Some of the greatest poets, scientists, and other scholars in the medieval Islamic world came from Persia.

Persia remained more or less independent in the modern era, occupying a tenuous position between East and West. Many of the inhabitants of Iran's largest cities were Western in outlook, while the country folk tended to be more pious Muslims.

The Pahlavi Dynasty ruled Iran for most of the 20th century and when Mohammad Reza Pahlavi became Shah (king) in 1941, he assumed the throne as a true dictator. He promoted a Western-style culture in Iran with repressive political policies. By the 1960s, the Shah had enemies everywhere: leftwing urban intellectuals hated him for his repressive tactics and fundamentalist Muslims hate him for failing to properly observe Islamic law.

It was only a matter of time before the Shah was brought down.

Khomeini spent most of his adult life working as a teacher and Islamic scholar, acquiring quite a reputation in those fields but never really being interested in politics. After all, the Shah never impinged on the field of Islamic scholarship and gave at least token recognition and respect to Shia Islam, so it was never a concern.

But then the Shah instituted a series of reforms beginning in 1963 known as the "White Revolution." Most of the White Revolution was benign as far as Khomeini and other fundamentalists were concerned, but reforms that gave women the right to vote and allowed non-Muslims to hold elected office made the Shah an enemy of the fundamentalists.

And Khomeini became the leader of the religious opposition.

Khomeini's leadership landed him in prison, and then exile, in 1964, making him a man without a nation for more than 15 years. He lived in Iraq for several years, before he came to the attention of the dictator 'Saddam Hussein', who wanted him gone due to his leadership of the Shia community.

As the Shah's repression in Iran grew, though, his control over the country slipped. He was overthrown in October 1979, which allowed Khomeini to return home and usher in a new era.

A Wonderful Valentine!

There is plenty of irony in the Khomeini's crazy decision to issue a fatwa on Salman Rushdie's life. Although Rushdie was raised in a Muslim family in India, he was a true citizen of the world, spending most of his time in Britain. He was not a practicing Muslim. Rushdie was a committed member of the Western leftwing intelligentsia class and as such was deeply opposed to the Shah of Iran.

Rushdie, like the leftwing in Iran at the time, even supported the Islamic Revolution in Iran and Khomeini initially. The writer and others like him thought, or hoped, that the new government would be authentically Persian, free of Western influence.

Well, they got their wish, but it didn't end up being the Utopia they wanted.

Yes, Iran was free of American influence and was authentically Persian, but it was also a theocracy that actually reversed most of the Shah's more liberal policies. Then Khomeini decided to imprison or kill the enemies of his new state, which included all the "godless communists" on the leftwing.

By 1988, Iran was already pretty much the biggest rogue state in the world, but when Rushdie's *The Satanic Verses* was published, it became even more so.

And really, the book isn't that big of a deal. *The Satanic Verses* is a fictional story about Indian ex-pats living in modern

England. In case you're wondering, it really doesn't have anything to do with Satan, but gets its name from a story that claimed the devil tricked Muhammad into adding three verses to the Quran before the prophet realized what had happened and eliminated them.

There were other elements of the book that were offensive to fundamentalist Muslims as well, such as many of the names of the characters and some of their seemingly immoral activities.

The negative reaction to the book was immediate. *The Satanic Verses* was banned in several Muslim countries and book stores in the United Kingdom and the United States. Some other countries that carried it were threatened and even firebombed. The stores that did carry it often kept it stowed away behind the counter.

Then Khomeini issued his famous fatwa on February 14, 1989. The Iranian leader probably didn't intend for the fatwa issuing date of Valentine's Day to have any sort of significance, but it was certainly taken that way. Not only did Khomeini call for any and all Muslims of the world, Shia and Sunni, to kill Rushdie for his blasphemy, but it also came with a $6 million bounty!

The fatwa had immediate repercussions throughout the world.

A new round of kidnapping of Western journalists in Lebanon by Shia militants took place, and for a time, Sunnis also seemed to rally around Khomeini.

The fatwa may have made Khomeini the most recognizable leader in the Islamic world, but its long-term effects for Iran were for the most part negative. Britain ended its official relations with Iran after the incident, which further isolated Iran. Even after Khomeini died in June 1989 and the Iranian government made attempts to appear more moderate, the crazy decision to issue a fatwa over *The Satanic Verses* continued to hover like a black cloud over Iran's foreign policy.

The fatwa on Rushdie's life is still in effect.

DID YOU KNOW?

- Although Islamic law would've permitted Khomeini to have up to four wives, he was only married to one woman, Khadija. They had four children; their two daughters, Zahara and Farideh, were actually accomplished scholars.

- Khomeini was a follower of the "Twelver" branch of Shia Islam. Twelvers believe that there are 12 imams, the twelfth of which lives in hiding and will only reveal himself in the end times.

- Rushdie survived an assassination attempt in London on August 3, 1989, when a Lebanese bomber blew himself up while making a bomb intended for the author.

- A Sunni Muslim terrorist group, 'al-Qaeda' added Rushdie to their long hit list in 2010.

- Khomeini and Saddam Hussein may have been bitter enemies, but they both shared hatred of the Kurds. Khomeini believed that their desire for autonomy divided Iran, so he sent troops to occupy their region and had their leaders arrested and killed.

NIKITA KHRUSHCHEV:

YOU CAN'T GROW
CROPS IN SAND

As far as dictators go, Nikita Khrushchev was definitely far less brutal than many of the men in our book. It helps that he took the reins of power in the Soviet Union right after Stalin died in 1953—definitely anyone would look less brutal after him, right?

Khrushchev was also far more diplomatic than his Soviet predecessor. He visited the United States in 1959 on a goodwill tour and, after the tense Cuban Missile Crisis in 1962, agreed to install the "red phone" in the Kremlin to avoid any possible nuclear misfires.

He also presented himself quite differently to the world. Unlike his predecessor, Khrushchev usually wore Western-style suits instead of military uniforms or worker's outfits and he wasn't afraid to show emotion.

Khrushchev also closed down many of the Stalin era gulags and reversed many of Stalin's repressive policies.

With all of that said, Khrushchev was still a dictator and a dictator who made some truly crazy decisions.

Perhaps the best-known crazy Khrushchev decision was to place Soviet missile bases in Cuba in 1962, which of course is what lead to the Cuban Missile Crisis. Thankfully for the world, that decision didn't end up going sideways, but an even crazier decision he made in 1954 did have long-lasting negative consequences for the USSR and Khrushchev.

The USSR was a big country, but the problem was that much of that land was too cold, the soil was poor, or it was too wooded to be good for farming. As a result, the Soviets were usually forced to import grain and other crops. Ukraine was the breadbasket of the USSR, but it still wasn't enough to feed the entire country.

So Khrushchev looked to the steppe of southeastern European Russia, north Kazakhstan, and west Siberia as a new location of cropland.

Khrushchev announced that the Soviet Union would employ a combination of state-of-the-art farming technology and thousands of volunteers to turn the steppe into farmland. He dubbed the program the "Virgin Lands" project and at first, it seemed to work. But after a while, logistical problems, poor soil, and uncooperative weather combined to doom the Virgin Lands to obscurity, making it the craziest and worst decision Khrushchev made as dictator of the Soviet Union.

When all was said and done, the USSR was left importing even more grain than they did before and Khrushchev was driven from office in 1964.

Little Nikita

At only 5'3, Nikita Khrushchev was never the type of imposing figure who could take over a room with his physical presence. Khrushchev was, though, a politically cunning and truly "Machiavellian" individual.

Born and raised in Ukraine, Khrushchev joined the Bolsheviks and became a political commissar during the Bolshevik Revolution and the Russian Civil War. After the communists claimed victory in 1922, Khrushchev had secured himself a nice spot in the Communist Party.

After Stalin came to power, Khrushchev became one of his willing henchmen. Khrushchev helped organize the purges that sent millions to the gulags and he even played a major role in the Holodomor, which of course left millions of Ukrainians dead.

For his service to the Motherland, Stalin rewarded Khrushchev by making him the head of the Communist Party in Ukraine. It was definitely a major promotion that put him on track to possibly succeed Stalin, but it was also a position that came with a lot of responsibility. And a lot of death.

The only thing that stopped Stalin's show trials, purges, and executions was World War II, which actually helped to elevate Little Nikita even more politically.

By the time the Soviets had driven the Axis forces out of the Soviet Union, the country was a mess, so Khrushchev was tasked with rebuilding Ukraine's agricultural and industrial infrastructure. After succeeding in the task, Khrushchev moved about as high as he could go within the government.

But then Stalin died in 1953.

Khrushchev knew that he had to act fast if he wanted not only to land the top spot in the Soviet government but also to survive. He worked quickly, having his top rival, Lavrentiy Beria, arrested and executed. It was a situation where the first one to blink died, and Beria blinked.

With Beria out of the way, Khrushchev was able to take over rule of the USSR and initiate his vision for the country, no matter how crazy it may have been.

The Virgin Lands Campaign

Once the Virgin Lands Campaign was fully outlined in 1954, Khrushchev sent thousands of tractors and combine harvesters and tens of thousands of young communist volunteers from Moscow and other parts of European Russia to the steppe.

Despite the sandy soil of the steppe, the first year saw excellent harvests and, by 1956, it looked as though Khrushchev's utopian vision would become a reality. Grain output and the cultivatable land increased more than 50% higher than the Soviet average before the program. The amount of money invested in the program returned a profit and it looked as though the USSR would become self-sufficient in terms of food.

But then crop failures hit in 1957 and it was all downhill after that until the program was canceled in 1963.

The Virgin Lands Campaign may have been a visionary idea, but it suffered from myopia, poor planning, and the failure to consider history and geography.

Although the program was hailed as a revolutionary method of doing agriculture, the planners failed to consider the most basic of farming methods. Fertilizers were rarely used to replace the nutrients in the soil, crop rotation and irrigation weren't implemented, and the machinery used was often inadequate or even obsolete.

The "farmers" who were sent to work the fields were unfamiliar with the machinery, often didn't have farming backgrounds, and were undersupplied by the government.

But what made the Virgin Lands Campaign the craziest decision of Khrushchev's tenure was that he totally disregarded the history and geography of the region.

The climate of the steppe is generally dry, which became apparent during droughts in 1955, 1957, and 1958. On the other hand, when storms do hit the steppe, they can be quite severe, sending the topsoil into the air and creating a "dust bowl" effect, which is what happened in 1960.

Above all, Khrushchev should have been able to take a quick glance at history to see that the steppe rarely produced farmers. The people of the steppe were historically nomads and pastoral people, moving with their herds from place to place.

If the Virgin Lands Campaign had have succeeded, there is little doubt Khrushchev would have kept the top post in the Soviet Union until his death, but it was an economic and political failure, and was one of the reasons the Communist Party removed him from office on October 14, 1964.

Khrushchev was allowed to live out his retirement peacefully until he died in 1971 at the age of 77, but he was said to be a shell of a man.

It all came about because Khrushchev tried to grow crops in sand!

DID YOU KNOW?

- Although Khrushchev was raised in Ukraine and spent most of his life there, he was an ethnic Russian.

- Khrushchev had a tenuous relationship with Stalin. Although he was one of Stalin's favorites, he was still subject to humiliation by the dictator: Khrushchev claimed that Stalin once made him do a traditional Ukrainian dance.

- Khrushchev married three times: his first wife died after only a few years of marriage, he divorced his second wife, and he remained married to his third wife, Nina Kukharchuk, until his death.

- Another major logistical/planning problem of the Virgin Lands Campaign was the lack of granaries and other storage facilities. Not enough granaries were built in the region of the Virgin Lands and since they were relatively isolated, transporting large harvests quickly to the more populated areas in Europe became difficult, leaving many harvests to rot in the fields.

- The young people who volunteered to work in the Virgin Lands Campaign were members of the All-Union Leninist Young Communist League, more commonly known as the Komsomol.

SAPARMURAT NIYAZOV:

NO LIP SYNCHING
ALLOWED, PEOPLE

If you've heard of the country of Turkmenistan, you're ahead of the curve by about 90%. That isn't to say that Turkmenistan isn't a great country and that its people aren't wonderful, just that the central Asian nation isn't really known for much other than being the fourth-largest producer of natural gas in the world.

The former Soviet republic is actually quite large in size at nearly 190,000 square miles, but it's sparsely populated with only just over six million people. Located just to the north of Iran, it was once in the middle of the famed Silk Road in the ancient and medieval periods of world history, but in modern times, it is best known for being one of many republics in the USSR.

More recently it became known for the man who ruled it with an iron fist from 1990 to 2006, Saparmurat Niyazov.

Saparmurat Niyazov was a relic and holdover from the Soviet era, who was the "Chairman of the Supreme Soviet of the Turkmen SSR" when it was still part of the Soviet Union, and then independent Turkmenistan's first president.

Niyazov's rule was straight out of the handbook of "communist dictatorships 101" in many ways, but he added several unique Turkmenistani touches. He cultivated an image that drew on a combination of influences—Soviet-era dictators, Islamic strongmen, and ancient Turkish traditions—which he related in his 1994 autobiographical book *Ruhnama*.

But the craziest things he did were his arbitrary decisions to make some seemingly mundane and innocent things illegal.

For starters, lip-syncing was banned at concerts, dogs were forbidden to enter the capital city, and he changed the word "bread" in the Turkman language to his mother's name.

And that was just the start of the crazy things Saparmurat Niyazov did while he ruled Turkmenistan. To be honest, none Niyazov's crazy policies really had the long-ranging negative effects that most of the other dictators' crazy decisions in this book have had. However, there were just so many of them and they were so interesting and humorous that there was no way we couldn't include him in this book!

Life Was Tough

Not much is known about Saparmurat Niyazov's early life up until the early 1960s. He was born in 1940 in the Soviet republic of Turkmenistan and was raised in an orphanage. Life was tough for kids in Soviet orphanages, especially in the lean years immediately after World War II. Scarcity was a way of life and death was a constant occurrence.

As Niyazov entered his teens, he saw that the only way to live a good life then was to be a member of the Communist Party. Niyazov was never the communist ideologue that many of the dictators we've profiled were; in fact, he was never much of an intellectual at all.

By all accounts, he joined the Communist Party to have a better life, but by the time the Soviet Union collapsed in 1991, he was the big man in Turkmenistan.

And Niyazov wanted to remain the big man.

He arranged it so that he would become independent Turkmenistan's first president in 1991. Niyazov was re-elected in a rigged "election" in 1994. All pretenses of the country being a democracy were dropped when the parliament declared him "President for Life" in 1999.

Then things really got crazy.

Who Needs Libraries?

As crazy as Niyazov may have been in many ways, he was smart enough to know that that the newly independent Turkmenistan would need a post-Soviet identity. So he wrote *Ruhnama*, which was part autobiography, part pseudo-history, and part political diatribe. It rambled and rambled and probably put more people to sleep than it inspired, but reading the book was one of the requirements for getting a driver's license in Turkmenistan.

Niyazov was known best for his crazy and often contradictory prohibitions of various activities.

Niyazov said he wanted to promote health and good values, so he banned smoking and tobacco use, but he also banned beads, which angered many men in the overwhelmingly Islamic country. His ban on dogs in the capital city was applauded by many fundamentalist Muslims, but few agreed when he closed all the libraries in the country.

At one point he even closed all the hospitals outside the capital city of Ashgabat with the idea that everyone should come to the capital for treatment. He also changed the oath in Turkmenistan to be an oath to the president.

But it doesn't end there!

Niyazov also banned internet cafes, the opera, ballet, circuses, women wearing makeup on television, and gold teeth. He claimed that all of these were bad influences and not proper activities for Turkmans to do.

Saparmurat Niyazov's ride on the crazy train may not have had the devastating effects on his country that some of the other cases we've profiled in this book did. Despite this, he was the victim of an assassination attempt on November 25, 2002. A shooter opened fire on his car in the capital that day, but no one was ever arrested. Many think it was related to some of Niyazov's shady business deals, but it could have just as easily been related to one of his crazy policies.

Maybe it was an angry healthcare worker who lost his job when Niyazov put 15,000 people out of work.

Or it could've been a disgruntled librarian who lost her job.

And maybe, just maybe, it was an angry lip syncer who wasn't able to freely engage in their favorite pastime.

Unfortunately, it looks like the identity of Saparmurat Niyazov's attempted assassin will never be known because after he died on December 21, 2006, the country quickly moved on without him.

The hospitals and libraries were reopened, and most importantly, the ban on lip-syncing was lifted!

DID YOU KNOW?

- *Ruhnama* is widely available online in PDF format or if you want a hardcopy for your library, you can pay $10 on Amazon.

- After the attempt on his life, Niyazov had more than 2,000 people arrested on a variety of charges. Most were released after short detentions.

- It is believed that Niyazov had assets worth more than $3 billion in cash and various investments around the world. Not bad for a former communist!

- Niyazov married his wife Muza when he was a student in Leningrad (St. Petersburg) in the late 1960s. They had two children together and remained married until his death.

- Although Turkmenistan may have moved on past Niyazov, the government still follows many of his repressive policies. The many gold statues that Niyazov had erected of himself throughout the country, especially in Ashgabat, are still there to greet all Turkmans and visitors to the country.

YAHYA JAMMEH:
CONDUCTING A WITCH HUNT, LITERALLY

Yahya Jammeh doesn't seem like a cruel despot when you first see pictures of him or hear him talk on video. The ebullient African usually had a smile on his face, was often dressed in traditional African garb, and generally didn't seem menacing at all.

So, how much of a threat could he be?

Jammeh was the dictator of the small West African country

known as The Gambia from 1994 to 2017. You should use the definite article "the" before the name of the actual country, or at least, that's what Jammeh dictated when he was in power.

There are only just over two million people who live in The Gambia and it really doesn't have much power in the world or even within the region of Africa, for that matter. Because of those reasons, most people just ignored Yahya Jammeh as another kooky African dictator, and for years so too did the other leaders of Africa.

But Yahya Jammeh eventually got too crazy even for Africa.

In January 2009, Jammeh's beloved aunt died, which left him reeling and looking for answers. Instead of going through the normal stages of grief as most of us do when we lose a loved one, Jammeh decided that he'd stall at the "blame" stage and focus on witchcraft as the target of his ire.

Yes, you read that correctly—Jammeh blamed his aunt's death on witchcraft and, as a result, he embarked on a violent campaign from mid-January to March 2009 to rid The Gambia of witches.

It was a literal witch hunt that left hundreds dead and nearly 2,000 people imprisoned. Others were tortured and raped while they also administered the hallucinogenic drug known as *kubee jaroo* to get the suspected witches and wizards to confess.

When the smoke of the witch hunts cleared, some Gambian villages were all but depopulated, hurting the already fragile economy of the developing nation.

The witch hunts also led other African leaders to reassess their relationship with Jammeh. Being a dictator was one thing, but they reasoned that the witch hunt incidents just made them all look superstitious and primitive. It proved to be one of the reasons why they removed him from power.

Jammeh's witch hunts were truly crazy and in addition to hurting the Gambian economy, they led to his downfall from power, for which many Gambians are grateful.

Learning the Tools of the Trade

Yahya Jammeh was born to a Muslim family in a small village in The Gambia in 1965, showing academic promise in school as a child. But like many countries in sub-Saharan Africa, The Gambia is a place where things can change fast and the only constant is the military. In countries such as The Gambia, the military represents stability and offers village boys the chance to move ahead in society.

So Jammeh joined the Gambian National Guard and then the Gambian National Army.

Jammeh learned first-hand that life in the Gambian military could be tough and was often violent, as punishments for indiscretions resulted in beatings or worse. It was also a perpetually corrupt institution, but that part of it never seemed to bother Jammeh.

In fact, he seemed to excel in the environment of violence and corruption, so much so that he helped lead the 1994 coup d'état against The Gambia's democratically elected president.

From that point forward, Jammeh was the leader of The Gambia in one form or another. And it was truly one crazy ride until he was removed from power in 2017.

Although Jammeh allowed "free elections," they were free in word only. Jammeh relied on government intimidation, ballot stuffing, and intimidation of his political opponents to win every election.

To keep the country in line with his crazier policies, Jammeh controlled the press and if that didn't work, he sent his paramilitary goon squad known as the "Green Boys" to intimidate the people.

And if there were especially tricky people who needed to be assassinated, Jammeh called in his professional hitmen known as the "Jungulers."

Jammeh's methods of repression were actually quite successful, but eventually, his level of craziness became too much.

The Greatest Witch Hunt of All Time

It remains unknown if Jammeh actually believed his aunt died of witchcraft or if he merely took advantage of a situation.

Many Westerns educated with a healthy dose of cynicism would believe Jammeh played on the religious beliefs and superstitions of his people, but even if that's so, it doesn't necessarily mean he wasn't a believer himself.

As strange as the witch hunts may appear, it's important to know that they were actually well organized. Jammeh would focus on a village or town he believed was infested with witches—or his political enemies if you're a skeptic—and send in a contingent of his Green Boys to kidnap the suspects and force them to ingest a hallucinogenic drink.

Professional witch doctors were also always present to identify witches and to cleanse the surroundings of their evil.

Although many people were abducted and accused of witchcraft apparently at random, many police departments appear to have been targeted, leading cynics to point out that Jammeh simply used claims of witchcraft to eliminate more of his enemies.

It was all over by the spring of 2009 and the witch hunts were just another one of the many crazy things Yahya Jammeh had done during his rule of The Gambia.

The crazy witch hunts further destabilized The Gambia, which led to a coalition of African nations intervening and forcing Jammeh into exile on January 17, 2017.

But don't feel bad for Jammeh; he left The Gambia with a cool $11 million from the country's treasury and now lives in luxury in Equatorial Guinea.

DID YOU KNOW?

- Another crazy policy that Jammeh pursued related to HIV/AIDs prevention and awareness. In 2007, he introduced a treatment program that claimed HIV/AIDs could be cured with natural herbs and recommend patients to stop taking antiviral drugs.

- Jammeh has been married three times, with the second and third marriages being polygamous. Apparently, the second and third wives didn't like the arrangement, though, because they both divorced him and now live in the United States.

- Despite public hearings into the abuses of the Jammeh regime, the identity of the Green Boys and witch doctors are mainly unknown. The ingredients of the concoction given to suspected witches also remains a mystery.

- Jammeh acquired the rank of colonel in the military before he became the dictator. Like Gaddafi, Jammeh never promoted himself to general.

- Jammeh was militantly opposed to any gay rights in his country while in power, which is generally in alignment with most sub-Saharan countries.

SLOBODAN MILOŠEVIĆ:

LIGHTING THE POWDER KEG
OF THE BALKAN WARS

Yugoslavia was never a real country by most definitions. Yes, it had defined borders and a government, but most of its inhabitants never viewed themselves as "Yugoslavians."

Instead, they saw themselves as their ethnicity first—Croat, Serb, Bosnian, Slovene, or Albanian—and then, possibly, as Yugoslavs. The very concept of the Yugoslavian nation was artificial and contrived, which is why the nation-state didn't last very long and why trying to keep it intact, as dictator Slobodan Milošević tried to do, was such a crazy decision.

The nation of Yugoslavia formed in 1918 from the ashes of Austria-Hungary. It was initially a kingdom known as the Kingdom of the Serbs, Croat, and Slovenes, but it was usually just called "Yugoslavia."

Yugoslavia was occupied by the Axis Powers during World War II and after the war, it became a communist nation under the rule of Josip Tito.

Although a communist dictatorship, Yugoslavia was not a member of the Warsaw Pact alliance and was much more open than other Eastern Bloc nations, allowing foreigners to visit the nation and for its people to come and go.

But its combination of propaganda and repressive policies was hiding fractures not far beneath Yugoslavia's surface.

Although the three primary ethnic groups in the country— Croats, Serbs, and Bosnians—all spoke the same language and shared many cultural traditions, some major differences set them apart.

The Croats are Roman Catholic and identify more with the West, the Serbs are Orthodox Christians and have historically looked to Eastern Europe for inspiration, while the Bosnians are Muslims.

When communism collapsed throughout Europe in 1990 and 1991, Yugoslavia was not spared. Leaders of the various groups wanted to dissolve Yugoslavia peacefully, but Milošević opposed the move.

He had become the president of Serbia in 1987 and had his sights on running Yugoslavia, which wouldn't happen if the "country" broke up.

As Yugoslavia quickly broke up, sometimes peacefully while at other times through civil war, into its constituent parts, Milošević made the crazy decision of resisting the change.

The result was the Balkans Wars, which lasted from 1991 to 2001. The wars cost the lives of up to 140,000 and caused widespread displacement and a refugee crisis due to ethnic cleansing campaigns and civilian massacres by all sides.

Looking up to Tito

When the Axis Powers occupied the Balkans during World War II, it revealed that not only was the region a patchwork of ethnic groups but also that they had very different agendas at times.

The Croats clearly favored the Axis Powers and wanted to use them to establish a Croatian national state. Likewise, the Muslims generally supported the Axis Powers. The Serbs, though, viciously resisted the Axis troops, fighting them for the entire war as partisans.

Once the war was over and order was reestablished in Yugoslavia, the communists led by Josip Tito came to power. Tito was the sort of dictator who commanded the respect of his peers, East and West, and usually got the results he wanted.

Yes, he was a dictator, but he was able to rule the country's different ethnic groups relatively smoothly until he died in 1980.

Slobodan Milošević wanted to be the next Tito, but he was clearly not of the caliber of Tito!

Milošević was born in Yugoslavia during World War II, so unlike Tito, he never fought the occupiers. Instead, he made his mark and gained power the way many men of his generation did: through the university and then in the Yugoslav Communist Party.

Milošević became the leader of Serbia in 1989, but Serbia was just one part of Yugoslavia. He wished to return to the glory days of Yugoslavia when the Serbs pretty much ran everything, which would have meant that *he* was in control of everything. But the other nationalities weren't so willing to go back to the way things once were.

Resisting the Tides of Change

When the Berlin Wall came down in 1989, it marked the beginning of the end of communism in Europe. Every communist regime that crumbled did so peacefully for the most part, except Romania and Yugoslavia.

The Balkans Wars were essentially a series of wars that resulted in the independence of several nations and the breakup of Yugoslavia. Slovenia broke away first after a 10-day war with Yugoslavia, then Croatia got its freedom after fighting from 1991 to 1995.

The Bosnian War from 1992-1995 was perhaps the most brutal of the Balkans Wars, with ethnic cleansing and massacres being regular features. Finally, the Kosovo War in 1998-1999 resulted in NATO bombings of Serbia.

And at the center of all of this was the crazy decision by Slobodan Milošević to resist it all.

In his desire to rule all of Yugoslavia as Tito had done, Milošević worked against the social changes that were sweeping Eastern Europe at the time. He wanted to establish himself as the dictator of Yugoslavia. Perhaps a greater leader may have been able to keep it all together, but Milošević just wasn't that man.

The reality was that the tides of change were just too strong.

Milošević's crazy and arrogant decision to keep Yugoslavia together under his rule at all costs accomplished nothing other than the deaths of nearly 150,000 people. Although Milošević did become the dictator of Yugoslavia in 1997, it was a nation that only consisted of Serbia and Montenegro, and Montenegro would leave peacefully in 2006.

Milošević's decision to try to keep Yugoslavia together made him and his nation an international pariah.

The Yugoslav authorities actually arrested Milošević in 2001 and then he was turned over to international authorities to face trial on a range of charges, including genocide, in The Hague, Netherlands. Milošević died in his cell of a heart attack on March 11, 2006.

Although some were upset that the Serbian dictator who started the Balkans War never faced justice in this world, most in the Balkans were happy to move on and rebuild their countries and their lives.

DID YOU KNOW?

- Milošević married his wife Mirjana in 1971 and had a son and a daughter with her. The entire Milošević family was heavily involved with him in government and therefore became wanted by international courts. They fled to Russia where they were given refugee status.

- Milošević signed the Dayton Accord in Dayton, Ohio on November 1, 1995. It ended the Bosnian War and all fighting in the Balkans until the Kosovo War in 1998.

- The Bosnians became Muslims in the centuries after the Ottoman Empire conquered the region in the 15th century. They would take Christian boys from their villages as part of tribute payment and train them to become warriors known as *janissaries*.

- Milošević has often been described as a political opportunist: he used Marxist-communist ideology to get ahead early in his career and later turned to nationalism.

- Once he became the dictator of Yugoslavia, Milošević enacted several laws that made it illegal to criticize the government.

FRANCISCO MACIAS NGUEMA:
NO MORE FISHING

When World War II ended, things didn't go back to "normal" in the world. The United States and the Soviet Union became the two primary superpowers, replacing the British Empire in the process. The British had incurred massive wartime debts and just weren't able to keep their empire together.

The same was true with the French, Dutch, and Spanish. All of the major European colonial powers gave up most of their possessions in the years after World War II.

Among the countries that achieved independence after World War II was a tiny African nation named Equatorial Guinea.

The country only has about 1.3 million people, but it is one of Africa's largest oil producers, so it's been able to wield a bit of influence in its short history. It's a history that began in 1968 when it became independent under the rule of Francisco Macias Nguema.

Nguema was actually elected democratically in Equatorial Guinea's first and only free election.

After that election, it's been pretty much downhill for the African nation, with corruption, fraud, and repressive dictatorships being the norm.

When the Spanish relinquished their colony in 1968, they wanted it to be run by a leader who'd keep the oil flowing and retain relatively good relations with Spain, so they supported Nguema, who was of the Fang majority.

Little did they know, Nguema was filled to the brim with crazy. After taking office, he would do one crazy thing after another, which kept his people poor and eventually got him executed.

By the time Nguema was driven from power, he had exiled or murdered up to two-thirds of the country and made those who stayed live under some pretty crazy and draconian rules.

He banned the word "intellectual" from public use and ordered the people of the country to change their first and surnames from Spanish to traditional African names. He also changed the country's motto to "There is no other God than Macías Nguema."

But Nguema did have a sense of humor...sort of. On Christmas Eve 1969, Nguema had assassins dressed in Santa Claus outfits murder 150 of his political opponents in a soccer stadium.

Now that's crazy!

Violence Begets Violence

Nguema's early life was as tough as any other dictator in our book, probably tougher. He was born into poverty in the Spanish colony of Equatorial Guinea and about the only thing he had going for him was being from the majority Fang tribe.

The Fangs were generally utilized by the Portuguese and then the Spanish to run things for them, so they had certain privileges, but Nguema's family was a bit more traditional and not so privileged.

Nguema's dad was a witch doctor who sometimes ran afoul of the Spanish authorities, which eventually cost him his life when he was beaten to death by a Spanish official. Young Francisco watched the brutal attack, leaving him with a deep hatred of the Spanish and a lesson in violence and brutality.

To make matters worse, Francisco's mother committed suicide a short time later.

Nguema was a persistent and resilient young man, although not necessarily the brightest. He had difficulties making it through school, but once he did, he rose quickly in the colonial government and became a mayor.

When it was announced that the Spanish were handing power over to the natives, Nguema threw his hat in the ring and ran on a platform that should have warned everyone how crazy he was.

One of the major planks of his platform was that he would take all of the Spaniards' homes and women and give them to his fellow countrymen. He also stated that Hitler was great for Africa and that he would Africanize the country.

Nguema won the election in a landslide.

Rule by Machete

Once Nguema took his oath as the president, it didn't take long for him to start his crazy programs. There really isn't one particular crazy thing he did that hurt him and his country; pretty much every policy he enacted was totally crazy and totally destructive.

The machete was Nguema's best friend and anyone who didn't follow his crazy decrees and directives was often hacked to death or at least lost a limb.

By the mid-1970s, things had become so bad that citizens of Equatorial Guinea were leaving by the thousands across the borders to Cameroon or Gabon. The best and brightest were leaving Equatorial Guinea by the droves and the skilled Guineans who didn't leave were often killed.

So, to stop his country's brain drain, Nguema decided to ban all boats and fishing. The boat ban was to stop people from sailing away, while the fishing ban wasn't as readily explained.

It probably had something to do with fishermen being close to the ocean and having access to boats, but it may have just been another one of Nguema's capricious, crazy ideas.

The end result was that, without skilled workers, the oil-rich nation had problems selling its valuable product, creating immense poverty. The ban on fishing made things worse for the poorest, who couldn't even fish for subsistence under Nguema's decree.

Finally, in 1979, Nguema's craziness was too much for the people of Equatorial Guinea (those still left anyway), so they overthrew him on August 3, 1979.

His trial began on August 18 and when he was convicted on September 29, 1979, he was also executed.

DID YOU KNOW?

- Nguema was responsible for the deaths of up to 400,000 of his own people, which when considered per capita makes him about the worst mass murderer in history.

- The crimes Nguema was charged with included genocide, murder, treason, and embezzlement. It turned out that Nguema was looting the profits from his country's lucrative oil reserves and putting the cash in banks around the world.

- Knowing that something was about to happen, Nguema sent his three oldest children to North Korea, where they escaped his fate.

- Nguema was a heavy user of the drugs *bhang* and *iboga*, to which some people attribute his paranoia.

- Like Pol Pot, Nguema targeted those wearing glasses for persecution, imprisonment, torture, and even death.

FERDINAND MARCOS:

THE WIFE REALLY LIKED SHOES

We've seen how some dictators were able to successfully navigate the often-precarious world of the Cold War era and use it to their advantage. Some of these smaller nations in Africa, the Middle East, and Latin America would cozy up to the USA or USSR to get favors, while outwardly professing a Marxist or capitalist world view.

Most of these dictators were more interested in power than anything, but they always tried to maintain some type of ideological pretense.

This wasn't necessarily the case with Ferdinand Marcos and his wife Imelda. True, Ferdinand was a capitalist and was very anti-communist, but that was mainly because he was afraid the communists would take the billions he milked from the Filipino people. He didn't really care about raising his people out of poverty; it was all about him and making sure his wife had enough shoes.

Ferdinand Marcos may not have been the most repressive dictator and he was actually popularly elected, but he was probably the greediest of all our dictators in this book.

It was Ferdinand and Imelda's Marcos' crazy desire to pursue wealth and hedonism that nearly led to civil war in the Philippines and sent the couple into exile. When the veil was finally lifted on the Marcos' corruption, it was truly staggering.

They had plundered the Philippines of between five and ten billion dollars' worth of money and property, which they used in a variety of investments around the world.

Then there were those shoes.

Imelda used her share of the plundering to go on lavish shopping trips around the world, buying expensive jewelry and designer shoes. By the time her husband was driven from power, Imelda had amassed a collection of more than 3,000 shoes, costing the Filipino people millions of dollars.

We all know some women love shoes, but that was crazy. So crazy that it played a major role in her husband's removal from power.

A Conjugal Dictatorship

It's impossible to discuss the dictatorship of Ferdinand Marcos without also discussing his wife, Imelda. The two were inseparable after they married in 1954 and throughout Ferdinand's rule of the Philippines from 1965 to 1986. They no doubt loved each other, and they also no doubt shared a love of material possessions.

Ferdinand was born into a politically connected family in the American ruled Philippines in 1917 and from a young age, he learned the tactics to be a successful politician in the Philippines: bribery, graft, corruption and violence, to name a few.

Marcos claimed that, when the Japanese occupied the Philippines during World War II, he fought against them, first as a regular soldier and then as a guerilla. But not everyone is so sure about his service, with some believing that he even collaborated with the Japanese.

The possible collaboration didn't hurt Ferdinand's political career, as he rose quickly in the government, winning election after election until he was elected President of the Philippines in 1965. And he couldn't have done it without Imelda.

Imelda Romuáldez came from a wealthy and influential family, so when she and the upwardly mobile Marcos met, it was a match made in heaven or at a bank. They married in 1954 and began their ascent to the Philippines' highest office together.

Avaricious Despots

Ferdinand Marcos didn't officially become a dictator until he declared martial law in 1972 and after that point; he made a lot of truly crazy decisions. He severely curtailed the press and rounded up his political enemies whenever he could. At the top of the list of his enemies were Muslims and communists.

Since he was going after communists and kept a lid on anti-American sentiments, American President Ronald Reagan winked and looked the other way when Marcos committed not only repressive acts but also plundered the country's treasury.

The longer Marcos' dictatorship continued, the more power Imelda seemed to gain. She would often join her husband in public events wearing expensive designer dresses and shoes from New York, Paris, and London.

People in the Philippines began wondering how the first lady of their country could live so well when so many Filipinos were going without.

Still, Imelda's ostentatiousness continued and she apparently had no problem throwing it in the faces of the Filipino people.

By the early 1980s, it was becoming clear that the Marcos family was losing control of the country, so Ferdinand responded by having many of his opponents assassinated. He had some dropped out of helicopters Pinochet-style and others, such as opposition leader Benigno Aquino Junior, were shot in broad daylight in front of plenty of witnesses.

The open violence was bad enough, but it was the crazy spending habits of Imelda and the couple's combined greed that brought them down.

Their looting of the Philippines treasury was so complete by the mid-1980s that it led to an economic collapse at a time when the world economy was doing quite well. In fact, since the Philippines' economy is often so heavily connected to the American economy due to the American military bases in the country and the large number of Americans and Filipinos who travel between both countries, economists were at first perplexed that the Filipino economy was performing so poorly.

But then they looked at Imelda's shoe collection and opened the books. People were amazed to find that the Marcos family owned luxury homes and apartments in the United States and that the first lady had jewelry and art collections that would put the Louvre to shame.

It was all too much for most Filipinos. A movement known as the People Power Revolution formed in 1986 to drive the couple from power, and once it became obvious how corrupt they really were, even President Reagan told them to take a hike.

The Marcos family fled to Hawaii where they were allowed to live in exile, sans most of their billions.

DID YOU KNOW?

- Ferdinand died in 1989 in Hawaii but was interred in the Philippines. Perhaps time does heal all wounds because Ferdinand and Imelda Marcos are remembered fondly by many Filipinos. Imelda is still alive and was allowed to return to the Philippines in 1991.

- Imelda and Marcos had three children and adopted one child. Two of their three biological children went into the family business of politics.

- The term to describe the joint rule of Ferdinand and Imelda, "conjugal dictatorship," was first coined by Primitivo Mijares in his book *The Conjugal Dictatorship of Ferdinand Marcos and Imelda Marcos*. Primitivo later disappeared and his son, Boyet, was assassinated via a fatal helicopter ride.

- In a show of her popularity, Imelda held elected office in the Philippines after her return from exile.

- Ferdinand Marcos put the Philippines under martial law after a series of bombings in Manila. The bombings were blamed on Chinese sponsored terrorists, giving Marcos the justification to enact martial law, but some believe they were false flags he ordered so he could have the cover to go after his enemies.

JUVÉNAL HABYARIMANA:
MAKING THE PEOPLE
GET UP AND DANCE

All of the dictators profiled in this book made crazy decisions that cost millions of lives, destroyed countries, and usually led to the end of the dictator. Sometimes it was just one or two crazy decisions that had one major impact, but other times it was a whole series of craziness that gradually wore down the dictator and his country.

Rwandan dictator Juvénal Habyarimana is an example of the

latter.

You probably don't know much about Rwanda, but there's a good chance that you know all about the Rwandan Genocide that took place there from April 7 to July 15, 1994. During that time, the majority Hutu ethnic group killed from 500,000 to one million members of the Tutsi minority ethnic group in a brutal and well-organized campaign of genocide.

The genocide was tied directly to Habyarimana's policy and when he was assassinated, the genocide began the next day.

There's no doubt that Habyarimana enacted some pretty crazy policies while he was in power. He took the name "Kinani," which means "invincible," as a sign to all of his opponents that he wasn't weak.

He persecuted those who disagreed with him, controlled the press, manipulated elections to win by impossible margins, and ordered the people to dance and chant his name in elaborate political rallies.

All of those things may be crazy, but the craziest thing Habyarimana did was allowing tension between the Hutus and Tutsi to fester and grow. Habyarimana was very tolerant of the Tutsis early in his rule, but owing to pressures from Hutus, he progressively began to strip them of their rights.

The decision to dispossess the Tutsis of their rights proved to be disastrous because it led directly to his assassination, which set off the Rwandan Genocide.

Power Comes from the Barrel of a Gun

Habyarimana was born to an upper-class Hutu family in 1937. His background gave him the ability to travel and attend better schools throughout what was at the time colonial Africa, allowing him to make connections that he'd later use during his quick ascent to power.

Habyarimana was an excellent student, showing some academic promise in Belgian colonial schools. He also knew that, in Africa, it wasn't about what you knew.

It was all about who you knew, and how many guns you had.

Instead of pursuing an academic career and possibly studying in Belgium or France as many of the upper-class Hutus did, Habyarimana went into the army because he had dreams of moving up the political ladder. He knew that the Belgians wouldn't always rule his country and in 1962 that dream started to become a reality when Rwanda was granted its independence.

Rwanda's independence didn't come without some blood being shed, although it wasn't the ruling Belgians who were killed but the minority Tutsis. The Hutus always liked their position of preference and the Belgians repaid them by standing by as they wiped out enough Tutsis to take control of the government.

Habyarimana saw that violence worked and that no matter how crazy he acted, if he had the backing of the right people, he could attain power.

Not So Invincible

There is no doubt that Habyarimana was probably one of the sharpest leaders in post-colonial African history. He was certainly a despot, but he knew how to plan things out and play the long game. Every connection he made while in the military was all done with the ultimate goal of taking power.

Finally, in 1973, Habyarimana used those connections to overthrow the president and take that role for himself. Habyarimana ruled Rwanda for more than 20 years through a combination of building a cult of personality, intimidation, and fraud.

The trifecta of despotism certainly worked, but one other thing he did—or didn't do—that seemed to help was not stoking the embers of ethnic hatred.

Despite being in the Hutu majority, Habyarimana generally didn't call for attacks on the Tutsis, which went remarkably far to maintain stability in Rwanda.

But forces outside and inside the presidential palace were constantly trying to persuade Habyarimana otherwise. An anti-Tutsi movement known as "Hutu Power" was gaining strength in Rwanda in the early 1990s and Habyarimana's wife's family were also anti-Tutsi.

The apparent pressure was too much for Habyarimana, causing him to make the craziest and most fateful decision of his rule. President Habyarimana gave in to the hate and decided to discriminate against and persecute the Tutsis.

The Tutsis decided not to sit back, striking out by taking down Habyarimana's jet with a stinger missile...with him on board. The assassination immediately led to an orgy of rape and murder, many of them committed with machetes.

When the United Nations finally restored order in Rwanda, it was immediately clear that all the misery could've been avoided if Juvénal Habyarimana hadn't made the crazy decision to go after the Tutsis.

DID YOU KNOW?

- The first five years of Habyarimana's rule were done under the military, but in 1978, he changed the country to a one-party state. The ruling party was the National Republican Movement for Democracy and Development.

- Juvénal Habyarimana was generally favored, or at least tolerated, by the West during the Cold War for his anti-communist stances.

- Another crazy thing Habyarimana did was to invite Zaire military troops into Rwanda to help suppress a Tutsi guerilla group. The Zairian troops were more harmful than they were good, as they raped many Rwandan women, forcing Habyarimana to expel them from the country.

- Habyarimana's wife Agatha fled Rwanda after his assassination. She lived in different locations, fearful of the Tutsi-led Rwandan Patriotic Front killing her. She eventually moved to France but was denied political asylum. Later, the French government denied the Rwandan government's request to extradite and try her for genocide in that country. She currently is in legal limbo.

- Habyarimana survived an attempted coup in 1980.

HUGO CHAVEZ:

HE WAS NO ECONOMIST

The modern political theory of democracy is viewed almost universally as an improvement on the systems that came before it, but there are some obvious problems.

Obviously, one of the problems is that clever demagogues can find a way to manipulate the system, and votes, to come to power. Many of the dictators in this book came to power through coups or revolutions, but a few were elected more or less legitimately, often by appealing to fears and hatreds of the masses.

Another problem with the democratic system is that it often places political leaders in positions that experts should hold.

To get votes, politicians will often profess to be experts on, or at least knowledgeable about, numerous subjects.

Politicians with a little more foresight will actually hire experts on particular topics to help them make more informed decisions, while those who tend toward authoritarianism and megalomania will make the decisions themselves.

Our last dictator is an example of demagogue and a politician thinking he's an expert on things of which he has little knowledge.

Hugo Chavez was democratically elected as the President of Venezuela in 1998. He won the election through demagoguery, attacking rich Venezuelans and foreign investors, especially American companies. But to stay true to his word, Chavez made the crazy decision of trying to play economist.

And the results have been devastating.

The oil-rich Venezuela has always had money management problems, but as Chavez tried to micromanage the economy, things only got worse.

Due to his nationalization policies, foreign investments dried up but domestic spending continued. The answer was to print more money, which led to inflation and recession.

Seemingly oblivious to the economic disaster all around him, Chavez doubled down on the polices. By the time he died in

2013, Venezuela was experiencing growing inflation, which eventually grew to 1,000,000% by 2018.

Hugo Chavez made a lot of crazy decisions and said a lot of crazy things during his rule, but pretending to be an economist was certainly the worst.

Not Such a Poor Kid

Hugo Chavez liked to promote the idea that he grew up in poverty in the slums of Sabaneta, Venezuela. The reality is that he came from a middle-class family, but after Chavez became a committed socialist/Marxist, it was better for his followers to believe he had a background of poverty.

Chavez attended a military school, which is where he was introduced to Marxism. But unlike many theoretical Marxists who have historically populated university campuses around the world, Chavez also had a military background, giving him a unique perspective on leftist revolution.

He learned that theories were great, but that ultimately, power only came from a trigger. Chavez's time in the military proved to be very productive, as he made many useful contacts and had time to better formulate his world view.

Then, as with pretty much all of our dictators in this book, fate stepped in to set Chavez's life on a new course.

Chavez joined a leftist clique within the military that attempted a coup in 1992, which landed the socialist and many of his comrades in prison. As he languished in prison for nearly two years, the political tides in Venezuela changed again. As is so often the case when this occurs, this shift led to Chavez's release from prison.

Upon his release, Chavez built a political movement that Venezuela's poor flocked to join, catapulting him to the presidency. Chavez promised a "Bolivarian Revolution" that would transform Venezuela's economy, making it more equitable for everyone.

He sure transformed the Venezuelan economy, but instead of raising the poor to the level of the middle-class, he brought everyone down to the level of the poor.

I'll Just Print More Money

When you talk about Venezuela's economy, it's important to know that the country isn't suffering from a resource problem. Venezuela is one of the world's leading oil producers and is sixth among OPEC nations, so there should be plenty of wealth to go around.

No, Venezuela's problem has historically been corruption and mismanagement.

When it came to Chavez and the Venezuelan economy, he promised a lot of things to his constituents that he just didn't have the resources or knowledge to deliver.

As the Venezuelan economy descended into turmoil, Chavez was like a deer trapped in headlights. With backgrounds only in the military and socialism, the more Chavez tried to control the economy, the worse things got.

By the mid-2000s, Chavez was able to manipulate the government and economy to rule as a dictator. Of course, not everyone was happy.

Chavez's opponents organized strikes in the all-important oil industry, to which Chavez responded by firing all the striking workers and replacing them with his own, unskilled workers. As a result, the once-lucrative oil reserves began to diminish.

Like many dictators have done in similar situations, Chavez's answer was to simply print more money. By the time he died in 2013, the Venezuelan bolivar was essentially worthless, supermarket shelves were empty, and Venezuelans by the thousands were crossing the border into Colombia.

Hugo Chavez may have done a lot of crazy things during his presidency, but thinking he was an economist by far had the most devastating effects on the country.

DID YOU KNOW?

- Another crazy thing Chavez did was to support the terrorist group, the Revolutionary Armed Forces of Colombia (FARC). The support placed Venezuela on various lists of state sponsors of terrorism and ruined relations with neighboring Colombia.

- Hugo Chavez really liked to hear and see himself talk. He hosted a television show every Sunday called "Aló Presidente" on state TV. It was an unscripted show that could go on for hours, with Chavez discussing anything from Marxism to pop culture.

- Chavez was married twice. He had three children with his first wife, Nancy, and one with his second wife, Marisabel.

- Chavez was reported to only have slept two to three hours a day. He stayed awake by drinking up to 26 expressos a day and some said, chewing on coca leaves.

- Another strange thing Chavez did was to move Venezuela's time zone 30 minutes behind its normal time.

CONCLUSION

Dictators are generally viewed by most normal people as crazy, and rightfully so, as they've historically done a lot of crazy things. This book has revealed some of the craziest things that 30 of the most notorious dictators in world history have done and the repercussions those crazy decisions had on them, their countries, and the world.

You now know that some of those crazy decisions had to do with attacking countries that should never be attacked. Napoleon and Hitler learned the hard way—and should've known based on history—that Russia is probably best left alone, while Mussolini learned that the glories of ancient Rome are best left in the ancient world.

Other dictators made crazy decisions with their countries' food supplies. Pol Pot and Robert Mugabe created famines to punish groups within their countries, Kim Jong-Il chose bombs over food, and Nikita Khrushchev made the monumental error of thinking he knew something about farming.

But since this book is about some of the crazy sh*t dictators have done, it wouldn't have been complete without some of the craziest dictators in history. Idi Amin, Francois Duvalier, and Francisco Macius Nguema were three dictators who seemingly lived in a different world, totally detached from the reality that most of us inhabit. Those men made crazy decision after crazy decision, and if they hadn't brought so many people so much misery, they'd have been comical.

And that is the truly unfortunate part of this all.

As much as the antics of many of these dictators was truly crazy and at times funny, it's important to remember that their crazy decisions destroyed entire countries and cost millions of lives. Most of these dictators and their crazy decisions seem far removed in time and place to most of us, but it's only a matter of time until the next one makes our list.

He or she may already be leading a country somewhere...

Made in the USA
Coppell, TX
14 December 2020

45158285R00125